lacking nothing

lacking nothing

The YEAR I LOST MY ABILITY TO EAT *and* FOUND SATISFACTION IN CHRIST

Natasha Kennedy

BakerBooks
a division of Baker Publishing Group
Grand Rapids, Michigan

Published by Baker Books
a division of Baker Publishing Group
Grand Rapids, Michigan
BakerBooks.com

Printed in the United States of America

Library of Congress Cataloging-in-Publication Data

Names: Kennedy, Natasha author

Title: Lacking nothing : the year I lost my ability to eat and found satisfaction in Christ / Natasha Kennedy.

Description: Grand Rapids, Michigan : Baker Books, a division of Baker Publishing Group, [2026] | Includes bibliographical references.

Identifiers: LCCN 2026017164 | ISBN 9781540906052 paperback | ISBN 9781493465408 ebook

Subjects: LCSH: Kennedy, Natasha | Christian biography—United States | Fasting—Religious aspects—Christianity | LCGFT: Biographies

Classification: LCC BR1725.K437 A3 2026

LC record available at https://lccn.loc.gov/2026017164

Cover design by Joshua Hunt

Baker Publishing Group publications use paper produced from sustainable forestry practices and postconsumer waste whenever possible.

26 27 28 29 30 31 32 7 6 5 4 3 2 1

For my children

May you see Christ's work in me as a gift

contents

Eternal God, heavenly Father, you have graciously accepted us as living members of your Son our Savior Jesus Christ, and you have fed us with spiritual food in the sacrament of his body and blood. Send us now into the world in peace, and grant us strength and courage to love and serve you with gladness and singleness of heart; through Christ our Lord. Amen.

preface

This book tells the story of the first year or so when I lost my ability to eat and how I discovered that Jesus is the only food I have ever needed.

My esophagus died, and I am told it will never function again. Without peristalsis—my throat being able to move food through it—and with several other conditions at play, this means my life will be one on a liquid diet, with periods of time when I am hardly able to drink even clear fluid. I am forced to live a life of fasting, and every day I am forced to make a choice: Will I resist, or will I embrace it?

As I walk through life in a body that cannot swallow food, I will always experience the temptation to turn my head to the right or to the left, toward other pleasures or comforts to wash over my sadness or fill my emptiness. But this emptiness is my allotted suffering; it is my appointed opportunity to see Jesus fill the emptiness and be to me what he has always been, even if I didn't notice.

Eternal God, heavenly Father, you have graciously accepted us as living members of your Son our Savior Jesus Christ, and you have fed us with spiritual food in the sacrament of his body and blood. Send us now into the world in peace, and grant us strength and courage to love and serve you with gladness and singleness of heart; through Christ our Lord. Amen.

As I fought through starvation, depression, pain, and confusion, I found solace in the words of this prayer. It is the prayer our parish prays after we take communion, pulled from The Book of Common Prayer, and it has been my source of truth week by week, day by day, and minute by minute as I have battled constant hunger.

I will use this prayer as the outline for this book because it captures each step of my personal journey as I discovered just how necessary it is for me to hold fast to Jesus as my true source of life.

We all have our allotted road of trials. We all come face-to-face, at some point, with the brokenness of our world and the horror of evil. Whatever your road becomes, may you find Jesus there, just as I did. May my story be one that inspires and compels you to cling—hard—to who Jesus is in your suffering and, like Jacob, not let go until you receive your blessing. May you be reminded that, in the midst of your lack and your pain and your suffering, you have everything you need.

To the faithful Christian who is grappling with the void of loss; to the weary Christian who is scared to drink from the cup of suffering; to the terrified Christian who has been led through the valley of the shadow of death—this is my gift. This is my story. I give you a window into the year of my life where I was most empty, most bare, most helpless, and in the most pain. I welcome you into the season of my life that I wouldn't wish on my greatest enemy. I implore you to read it with a curious and hopeful heart, knowing that the same Jesus who met me, led me, and suffered with me during that time is the same Jesus who is with you. He is enough.

This book is a prayer. It is a prayer I must choose to pray every single day, because my trial is not going away. My need for Jesus will *never* go away, and I am reminded every day through this affliction how much I need him. It is my hope and my ambition: to be content and at peace and to trust that Jesus' body and blood—that his *word*—are enough.

1

chosen lack

Eternal God, heavenly Father, you have graciously accepted us as living members of your Son

"You will never swallow solid food again." It didn't matter how many times I heard the doctor's words, I could not believe them. Not me—the lover of all things creamy and delicious; not me—the jovial housewife who spent my evenings drinking wine while I cooked, dreaming of culinary school. Not me, the girl once nicknamed McTasha by friends who always spotted my yellow car at the drive-through. Surely, there was *something* that could be done! But there wasn't. At the age of thirty-three, my esophagus had died, and I didn't know why.

I love life. I live for the highs and the moments of pure happiness. I have a romantic view of the world, like a bard who writes songs that make the mundane look fantastic. Beauty is all around us, if we would only see it for what it is. I spin the threads of my everyday life into stories, so that I can point to a tapestry and say, "Look—isn't this amazing?"

It shouldn't come as a surprise that I write fiction. It also shouldn't come as a surprise that I sometimes view my own life like a novel, like a fantasy story with symbolism and climactic moments, reeling cliffhangers that keep you on the edge of your seat. Things as simple as changing diapers or driving my kids to the grocery store become fantastic, awe-inspiring events in my mind, making my life, in all its various forms, a pleasure to live. I've always taken joy in discovering where God fits into these stories, to let him be the ever-present melody that plays like a theme throughout my otherwise ordinary life.

So what do I do when my story descends cruelly into a cave—a hollow black pit of ugliness, barrenness, and confusion—one where I can't see a way out? Where is God when I see no happily-ever-after in my story, when the pain and the loss become so great that I find myself not wanting to walk deeper into the cave, fearing where it might lead?

How could a story this dark ever get better? *Does* it ever get better? What is the good end to a story where I never eat again? Where is the beauty in a world where I am told I might die young or live in constant pain? A bard may have the perfect song to sing to someone who is dying. But what does that bard sing to himself when *he* is dying? *Can* he sing? Can he believe the words of his own song?

Fasting, as I once knew it, was an unnecessary and unwanted practice of limiting myself. It was the act that took the bard's instrument away, forcing him to sit in silence. How could that be *good*? Why do that to myself when that lovely music was the only thing keeping beauty running like a clean stream of inspiration through my life?

Silence. It was the thing above all that I feared most. Silence, emptiness, want, and starvation.

What good could come out of a season of starvation and lack? The answer I have come to has been surprising: that this has been *more* beautiful, *more* real, *more* full, and *more* compelling than any other season of my life. The rose-colored glasses that I thought were making my experience of this broken world so much better were ripped cruelly from my face, and I was forced to *really* look at the world and test whether or not true beauty and goodness were surrounding me.

Food was one of those things I thought I couldn't live without. I mean, really, doesn't everyone believe that? Who could live without food? But I've found something that satisfies me even more than food. I have been forced to believe Jesus when he said he would be enough for me—to really stare into the void of what I thought I needed and find something so much better than I had before.

Until my diagnosis, I lived a life of "feasting." Until I lost the ability to eat, I hadn't realized that feasting isn't feasting until it is juxtaposed with fasting. But feasting without the presence of *fasting* is gluttony. I was a glutton—and I still am. What do I mean by that? I mean that as a glutton, I want so much happiness that I become bloated, overstuffed, and numb to the beauties I consume. Gluttons don't just eat what they need; they eat more. Gluttons don't reserve abundance for special times—times which I will refer to as "feasts" in this book—but they live a life so full of abundance that abundance becomes the norm.

I am the glutton who had abundance stripped away from her. This loss came like a thief in the night, stealing my most precious possessions, forcing me to see what I truly treasured.

How It All Began

Our family had only recently become Anglican. Craving spiritual grounding and structure, we joined our local parish and found novel enjoyment in framing our family's life and routine around the church calendar. As our very first Lent season approached, we chose to fast as a family, giving up meat for the forty days leading up to Easter.

I had grown up evangelical and was somewhat skeptical about the practice of fasting, but I was ready to try it and hoped to find meaning in the discipline that seemed so vital to Christ's life. We explained to our four children that it would be hard and long, but we relished the experience of doing something that was hard together. What we didn't expect was to enjoy it so much. Even after

Easter, our kids asked to fast again! What a perplexing thought: fasting being *enjoyable*. It felt so contrary to how I saw the world. Being a lover of rich, savory food myself, it was hard to imagine a world where saying "no" to those desires could be livable, let alone enjoyable.

Retrospectively, I see our family's Lenten fasting as a kindness, a season that would prepare me for the life to come. It is amazing to think that even my children had a frame of reference for what would happen to their mother later that year.

I had chosen to fast that Lent, but what happened after was not my choice.

It all started in May, just after Easter. I went into the local emergency room with steak stuck in my throat. It was the most horrifying experience; "choking while still breathing" is how I described it. With the esophageal blockage came pain—*indescribable* pain. This emergency room trip was followed by another, and another, and *another*. Food would not pass through my esophagus into my stomach. Finally, my case became urgent enough to be rushed to a specialist.

That was when we were told about esophageal dysmotility. I learned about how my esophagus wasn't just a tube but a muscle that moves food along when food and drink are swallowed. "Dysmotility" means my digestive system's muscles—in this case, my esophagus—weren't acting as they should: They were either underperforming (with no muscle contractions), overperforming (with repeated painful spasms), or a combination of both.

The diagnosis for such a disorder takes time, waiting, and some pretty difficult tests. As I went through the process of discovering just how bad the dysmotility was, I played the longest waiting game of my life: a two-month fast. Whether from stuck food, esophageal spasms, or intense swelling, from May to July, I could not eat *anything*. For much of the time, I could not even drink water. I was in the hospital regularly for IV fluids and nutrition, and when I wasn't there, I was at home trying to force tiny bits of liquid into my stomach, only to throw it up again.

I was starving. I was dying—and I didn't know why.

We all go through life knowing that death is a reality and that we will one day meet it, but we don't really believe in it. It's not until we actually taste the true nearness of death that we start to realize just how imminent it is. As Jean-Claude Larchet says in *The Theology of Illness*, "In times of illness the inevitability of death becomes a stark reality."[1] Up until then, we are seemingly immortal. It is the drunkenness of youth—the optimism of the healthy—that allows us to believe we can go on living happily ever after.

This was my moment of truth, the moment those rose-colored glasses were ripped from my face, the moment when I realized I was going to die. And then, suddenly, I was faced with my need for rescue.

I don't want to die. I hated having to say those words. I was supposed to be young; I was supposed to have years and years of not thinking about death. I wasn't *ready* to face this reality. *I can't die; I have four children—one of them only a year old! I can't die; I have only just started my illustration career! I can't die; there are so many things I want to experience!*

I found myself alone, starving, suffering, and confused. I needed rescue. I needed hope. *The Theology of Illness* went on to say, "Far from being an event that touches only our body, and that for a limited time, illness often forces us to assume a spiritual struggle that involves our whole being and destiny."[2] There had to be an answer—not just for my physical needs but for the attack on my life and future my disease had provoked.

My family chose to see this as a "forced fast," hoping to connect some meaning to my intense time of suffering. My husband, Lindsay, bought me a few books on fasting, and this spurred on an ongoing conversation that we still continue to this day. We found ourselves asking this question: *What if fasting is good?* What if—through this time of trial—there was treasure to be found? What if there was a richness that could be gained *only* through fasting?

Later on, during one of the days I felt too near to despair, Lindsay asked: "What if this isn't the worst thing that's ever happened to you—what if this is the most *special* thing about you?" If fasting was bad, then this is the worst thing that could have happened to me. But if fasting was good? Then perhaps Lindsay was right.

These questions brought me back to Lent, back to the story of Jesus in the wilderness. Jesus had *chosen* his time of fasting: forty days without eating in preparation for his time of temptation. My suffering had been experienced by Christ before, and he held the answers to my questions. I clung to this story, reading it over and over, reciting the words he spoke in the wilderness as if those very words kept me alive—and maybe they did.

> Man cannot live by bread alone, but by every word that comes from the mouth of God. (Matthew 4:4)

I had always thought I believed that verse. It wasn't until I *needed* it that I realized it was true. It wasn't food that kept me alive; it was the Word of God. A new hunger began inside me, one that could only be fulfilled by truth. Without the Creator of the world speaking life into my body, I would die. I didn't need food; I needed him. I needed to need him. I needed to believe I needed him.

Living Members of Christ's Body

There is a prayer that we pray after taking communion at our church. As a congregation, we say these words together, proclaiming our faith that by partaking in the sacrament of Jesus' body and blood, we have been "*fed spiritual food.*"

This prayer became a lifeline for me. Week by week, as I battled starvation, pain, and terror, I clung to these words, reciting them as an act of faith, hoping they would keep me alive.

The prayer begins with these words: "*Eternal God, heavenly Father, you have graciously accepted us as living members of your Son . . .*"

Jesus lived a human life on this earth, paving a way to salvation for us. In becoming part of Jesus' body, we get to take part in his life. Jesus suffered, so we will suffer; Jesus triumphed over temptation, so we will triumph over temptation; Jesus died, so we will die; Jesus rose from the dead, so we also will rise. My path to overcoming a life of suffering was first walked by Jesus, and that means something very, very comforting: I am not alone.

I was scared—and I still am to this day—of what this kind of loss and suffering will do to me. To be in this much pain, to not be able to eat solid food, to face an entire life struggling to swallow liquid to live is the sort of thing that breaks a person. To be a creature of suffering: that is my greatest fear. To be broken and disfigured by it; to succumb to the inhumanity of the pain, or to become useless to my husband, my children, and the world.

My only hope is this: to be like Christ in his suffering, so that I may partake also in his resurrection. The fear is real; the reality that I could one day be led to despair and hopelessness through my suffering is real. But I must remember that, with his Spirit inside me, I am one with Christ. If he suffered, I will suffer; if he died, I will die; if he rose from the dead, I will also rise.

> For his sake I have suffered the loss of all things and count them as rubbish, in order that I may gain Christ . . . that I may know him and the power of his resurrection, and may share his sufferings, becoming like him in his death, that by any means possible I may attain the resurrection from the dead. (Philippians 3:8, 10–11)

Pain should either be avoided or healed: Only these two options were available to someone who was living a full, healthy life in Christ. No one ever explicitly said those words to me, but those were the undertones in every conversation, every prayer, and every interaction where my physical struggles were addressed. I have had plenty of caring, well-meaning people tell me, "This just isn't right," or, "God doesn't want this for you," or, "You need to be healed."

Those words were meant to comfort, but instead they spoke into the lies that I had believed: that pain must either be avoided or healed. *This was not good; this was not from God; you should not be in pain; you need to be healed.* If that was true, then I was in big, big trouble. I was always in pain, and hearing that I shouldn't be didn't comfort me—it instead led me to guilt, condemnation, and isolation.

But what if there is *good* for the Christian who suffers? What if there are riches that can only be gained through this suffering?

What Is Fasting?

Fasting represents a missing piece in this theology. Fasting is a form of *chosen* suffering and *chosen* lack. It is the belief that there is good that comes from suffering and from limiting oneself, specifically in regard to food and drink. Fasting is a discipline practiced by Jesus, his followers, and Christians throughout all generations.

Some misconceptions and bad theology have scared people away from this practice, and none more so than me. I am sure that you have also heard at least one of the following reputations of fasting:

Fasting *is asceticism.*

Fasting *is unhealthy.*

Fasting *leads to shame.*

Fasting *is too hard.*

Fasting *is salvation by works.*

Fasting *is vain.*

Fasting *makes no difference.*

Fasting *leads to other temptations.*

Fasting *is inconvenient.*

Just like any Christian practice—from worship, to communion, to prayer, to teaching—fasting can involve unhealthy thinking or habits. But like worship, communion, prayer, and teaching, fasting should not be thrown out with the bathwater. It is discussed in Scripture as an *essential* part of the Christian life. Jesus not only fasted when he was on the earth, but even now, he is fasting:

> Now as they were eating, Jesus took bread, and after blessing it broke it and gave it to the disciples, and said, "Take, eat; this is my body." And he took a cup, and when he had given thanks he gave it to them, saying, "Drink of it, all of you, for this is my blood of the covenant, which is poured out for many for the forgiveness of sins. I tell you I will not drink again of this fruit of the vine until that day when I drink it new with you in my Father's kingdom." (Matthew 26:26–29)

We take communion in faith that he will return. But here, we see that *he* is fasting wine until we are all together. Jesus, even in paradise, is withholding wine from his lips.

I have heard people use the term "fasting" in many ways. It is commonly used as a word for "abstaining for a time." I believe that a feasting/fasting mindset can be applied to all forms of abstinence, and I truly believe that there are specific treasures and gems only to be gained by the practice of fasting and that they yield a greater harvest when it comes time to feast.

But in my story, I use this word exclusively with its original meaning: to abstain specifically from food or drink.

Fasting should not be a question of *should* but rather *how*. When Jesus spoke about fasting in his Sermon on the Mount, he didn't speak about *if* someone fasts but rather *how* they fast. Fasting is paired with prayer in Scripture and is historically seen as a transformative discipline. Fasting is good; fasting *should* be practiced. A life flavored with fasting sets us up for greater fulfillment. Fasting isn't just the experience of *lack*; it is the tender, quiet, and hopeful contentment that lack can produce that is the prerequisite for true, abundant fullness.

I was never the type to fast. I used every excuse possible in order to avoid making it a regular practice in my life. I hate denying myself, and I hate suffering. I did not understand how denying myself could truly be a good thing. Then, when suffering became a regular part of my life, I found myself needing to shift my mindset around it. Others in my life did not want to see me suffer either. Like me, they couldn't see any goodness in what I was going through. Friends' kindly meant words only reinforced the lie that suffering and lack do no good for the Christian.

Fasting presents the Christian with an alternate perspective. The practice of fasting is rooted in the belief that times of lack bring about something good. I don't mean to say that suffering in itself is good. Without Christ, suffering leads to nothing but death. But *in* Christ, we are told that our suffering brings us closer to him. This means that when we go through loss and pain, it is not a hopeless experience. No, Christ is able to turn our pain into something good. In him, pain is no longer just an evil thing. As Christians, we can have hope in the midst of our suffering, and just as Christ's death preceded his victorious resurrection, suffering precedes our present thriving and future glory.

> *Eternal God, heavenly Father, you have graciously accepted us as living members of your Son our Savior Jesus Christ, and you have fed us with spiritual food in the sacrament of his body and blood. Send us now into the world in peace, and grant us strength and courage to love and serve you with gladness and singleness of heart; through Christ our Lord. Amen.*

This prayer after communion helps me create a structure for my story and the beauty that has come through depending on Christ in my season of trial. I have gone into the wilderness—into the place with no food and barely any water—and I have found Jesus there. I have been nurtured by the bread of his word, and I have found contentment in a world without numbing or vices. My struggle is to remain in that place: like Peter, with his eyes fixed on Jesus, walking on water; like a glutton starving in a desert, staring at the face of Jesus.

In this place of dependency, I have found peace. In this place of suffering, I have found comfort. In this place of hunger, I have been satisfied. And in this place of terror, I have found hope.

In the wilderness of fasting, I have found Jesus.

2

into the wilderness

Our Savior Jesus Christ

Here is a little window into what my life was like before the crisis, a picture of my normal before *normal* was destroyed when this trial blindsided me and, like a hurricane, tore down everything that I thought home, life, and *normal* was.

Our family had just moved to the United States from Scotland. Lindsay had been pursuing a PhD at St Andrews, and while that idyllic quiet life in the small fishing village of Crail was beautiful, it was also isolating. The closest family lived two hours away, and the country was deep in Covid lockdown. I had just given birth to my fourth child, and we decided that we needed more stability. Therefore, we chose to move back to the Seattle area, where I grew up and where my husband Lindsay had a stable job. It was hard giving up the life we had in the UK, but we really believed that it was time to pursue *stability* over dreams.

Oh, stability—what a funny word. I am chuckling to myself as I write this, because I'm thinking about just how deeply Lindsay and I craved it. Our lives did stabilize in some areas, but other places were shaken deep at their foundations, and we were left reeling from the impact.

As we relocated to Seattle, we used Psalm 131 as a lens through which to look at our new, stable life:

> O Lord, my heart is not lifted up;
> my eyes are not raised too high;
> I do not occupy myself with things
> too great and too marvelous for me.

> But I have calmed and quieted my soul,
> like a weaned child with its mother;
> like a weaned child is my soul within me.
> O Israel, hope in the LORD
> from this time forth and forevermore.
>
> (Psalm 131)

I wanted a quiet soul. So much of my life I had been fighting and striving to just *arrive* at a quiet, content place. I no longer cared about accomplishments and ambition as much as just living a simple life. I wanted what the psalmist had—the contentment to just sit beside my Lord, wanting for nothing, asking for nothing, fully at peace.

After arriving in the Seattle area, I found myself asking: *Lord, please just give me what I need in order to be at peace.* We were a family of six, living in a two-bedroom apartment, struggling to stabilize amid the high cost of living in Washington state. I had asked the Lord for everything I needed in order to be at peace, and I had thought this would mean him giving me *more* than what I had access to. Instead, it meant *less*. Instead of giving me the physical provisions I imagined, he gave me something I never would have chosen for myself: He gave me fasting.

I am a children's book illustrator by trade. In the fall of 2021, I was working on the FatCat book *The Lord's Prayer: For All God's Children*. I remember waiting in the emergency room, my iPad in my lap, drawing. I had intense esophageal pain, which at the time felt something like heart pain. It would still be a few months before my esophagus completely stopped working, and so we were at a loss to know where this sudden onset of chest pain was coming from.

As I sat in the waiting room, I worked on sketching out and coloring a page from the Lord's Prayer book: *Lead us not into temptation*. In the picture, Jesus is sitting in the desert, surrounded by the hot sun, barren land, and vultures. He is also surrounded by onlooking angels, and there—in the middle of a forty-day fast—he sits, smiling. I thought to myself how ironic it was that I happened to be coloring that page while I was in the hospital, surrounded by the trial of my own confusion.

Imagine Jesus sitting in the desert, smiling, surrounded both by barrenness and angels. This was the picture that lingered in my mind as the pain and suffering grew worse and worse until the following May, when I couldn't swallow at all. I was surrounded by both barrenness and angels.

The Two-Month Fast

From the fall of 2021 to May 2022, my health seemed to decline at a disturbing rate. I found myself in that emergency room over and over again as the chest pain worsened and my ability to swallow decreased. We couldn't figure out what was happening, but Lindsay and I continually promised each other: *Soon this will pass, and we can finally stabilize.*

Leading up to that dark May, our family was taking part in our church's Lenten fast. We chose to give up meat as a family, except for on Sundays, which are considered feast days. The fasting/feasting dynamic was a new one for us. Until 2021, we only had been in evangelical circles, which, while excellent, lacked liturgy and practices such as fasting. Fasting and feasting introduced a new paradigm through which we viewed our days. Times of fasting gave us opportunities to find contentment in Jesus, the true source of sustenance, and times of feasting gave us opportunities to rejoice in the abundance of Jesus' blessing.

Lent was like a pleasant ride on an outdoor swing, swaying back and forth rhythmically between saying "no" and "yes" to abundance and pleasure. The juxtaposition between lack and abundance made each experience more satisfying. After church, we grabbed Happy Meals from McDonald's for the kids, and after a week of no meat, it made the treat seem so much greater.

The experience of fasting and feasting provided subtle undertones to our days and the way we lived our life. When fasting, it seemed so much easier and more natural to say "no" to myself when I felt indulgent impulses, and I felt so much more joy saying "yes" on feast days, because it was actually the *right* thing to do.

I could wax eloquent for pages and pages about how valuable liturgy and rhythm is for the Christian life, but instead, I want to zoom in on one aspect of Christian liturgy: the practice of fasting and feasting.

That entire season of Lent, I was working on illustrating *The King of Easter*, another FatCat book, which was due to be released the following Easter. On the first page of this book, Jesus is standing at an empty table, wondering whom he should invite to his feast. As the book continues, on each page, Jesus is seeking and saving people, and each of those people respond by following him. At the end of the book, we return to the image of the feast table, where everyone from the book is shown eating together and rejoicing. It was startlingly poetic that I illustrated the empty table spread at the start of Lent, worked on the main pages through the forty days of Lent, and then illustrated the final feast right in time for Easter.

As the season of Lent came to a close, our church body gathered together and welcomed Eastertide with a big feast, just like the characters in the book. The fast was over; it was time to celebrate! Jesus is risen: that is our feast. The eating of food and the indulgence of feasting was a representation of the truer feast: that we have abundance in Christ. We all fasted, suffering like Christ suffered, and then we all feasted, triumphing because Christ triumphed.

The following month was May 2022. I wound up in the emergency room again, this time with a piece of steak completely obstructing my esophagus. It happened so fast—so horrifyingly fast—and began my two-month period of starvation.

The best comparison I can make to that experience is the image of Jesus in the desert that I spoke about earlier. I was in a desert, surrounded by barrenness, and yet, I was not alone.

It was one of the scariest seasons in my life. Every day was a battle, trying and failing to get food into my stomach. Soon, even water would not go down. Everything I swallowed came back up; nothing could get through my esophagus. Rushed trips to the hospital became a regular rhythm of those two months, where I would get nutrition through IV fluids and tiny sips of broth. Every day, we would be told, *This will pass soon*. But it never did pass. It went on, and on, and on. During that first month I went through diagnostic testing for esophageal motility disorders. These are rare, specific tests, only offered by two hospitals in Washington state. There would be a long wait before results came in.

As I waited two months for those results, I battled starvation—*true* starvation. Intense hunger was a pain I had never experienced before. It was a pain I thought I could never endure, and yet, there I was, enduring it. It became so regular that I began to fear the idea of food in my stomach. Irrational ideas were introduced to my mind: the fear of eating food, becoming disturbed by other people eating food, and feeling comfortable with the sensation of an empty stomach. This suffering was not helped by the fact that my gastrointestinal doctor was not well-versed in GI motility, and she did not take my experience very seriously until after the results eventually came in. This made the wait more isolating—the implication that this must be all in my head. Nothing was "wrong," and yet I couldn't swallow.

And yet, something unexpected happened. I starved for two months, and as I did, I developed a taste for a certain kind of prayer that I had never before allowed myself to experience: prayer with fasting. I entered deeply into a place of dependency on Jesus. I discovered that *man does not live by bread alone, but by every word that comes from the mouth of God* (Matthew 4:4). Jesus gave me an example of how to fast, how to suffer, and how to depend fundamentally on God, rather than physical resources, for life. Jesus did it first, and he was the perfect guide to lead me through the wilderness of my lack.

Rescue from Gluttony

Before I could see Jesus as a provider during my season of lack, I first needed to understand what, exactly, I needed rescue *from*.

I am, as I have said before, a feaster. I never willingly withhold a feast from myself, unless it's one of those sporadic seasons of my life when I am trying some extreme diet in order to lose weight. And still, even while trying a weight-loss program, I am still a feaster. I am a lover of abundance, excess, pleasure, and mountaintop experiences.

And what is a feaster who never fasts? A glutton.

Before I say any more, I want to make something abundantly clear: being on the obesity scale does not equal gluttony, and gluttony is not the same thing as being on the obesity scale. For most of my married life, I have been on the obesity scale, and it all began with a severe hip injury, followed by having three babies, three years in a row, interwoven with the sadness of five miscarriages. A dreary cloud of depression hung over those years, along with times of intense loneliness. I refuse to feel shame about the effects that had on my body, and I exhort my readers to show themselves the same grace. Your body is yours—it is the physical representation of who you are, what you have been through, and how you experience living in this world. Your body is *you*, and *you* are lovely.

So, while I carefully use the imagery of body fat as I talk about the sin of gluttony, I do not mean to communicate that gluttony is obesity, or that obesity is gluttony. They can, however, be tied together symbolically, and that doesn't mean it has to cast shame on those of us who have been or are still technically overweight.

I was a glutton when I was a thin, active college student; a glutton when I was over two hundred pounds, depressed, walking with a cane, and pregnant; and I am a glutton now, rapidly losing weight and unable to eat. My definition of "gluttony" is the refusal to withhold from oneself an excess of the pleasures of this world. When I got a bundle of money from a book deal, I spent it; if my dad offered to buy me dinner, I ordered three courses and three drinks; if I had a bad day, I ordered takeout for dinner; if I felt stress about my life, I sat on the couch and binged my favorite show. If I wanted it, I took it.

Gluttony creates a cushion of comfort—a thick layer of fat—around ourselves, numbing and creating distance between our true self and the world we live in. The draw of gluttony isn't necessarily an addiction to pleasure as much as it is an addiction to using pleasure as a way to comfort and numb oneself. The world isn't so bad when I have a thick layer of comfort to protect me, in the same way that a cold outdoor experience isn't so bad when I have a thick layer of body fat to keep me warm. Fat distorts the true experience of being in this world, and I didn't truly realize it until I lost fifty pounds in only a few months.

I remember the chilling, terrifying, *sobering* feeling I had when I lost all that weight. I kept saying to Lindsay, "I feel so close to the world, so raw and exposed." It wasn't a nice feeling at first; it was scary. Gluttony makes us feel protected from the world, and *that* is why it is so addicting.

I don't think I'll shock anyone by saying that I think gluttony is the cardinal sin of our culture today. We live in a world full of advertising, preaching, customs, and events *all* centered around food, comfort, and fullness. Our world doesn't seem as scary with a fast-food restaurant on every corner; it doesn't feel as bad when we spend our evenings scrolling on our phones; it doesn't feel so hopeless when we have money to spend on new things. We are all addicts, all slaves to the need for comfort, because we truly believe that without these cushions, we will be lost.

This is why fasting always seemed so abhorrent to me. Why should I withhold fullness from myself? Without fullness, I can't live! Despite what I say in this book, I still struggle not to return to this lie: that I cannot be satisfied without comfort.

This glutton needed—and still needs—rescue. We cannot receive rescue until we believe we are in need of it. This is the moment where you stop and ask yourself: *Am I willing to be rescued from this richly gilded cage?* If it makes you feel any better, I wasn't. At least—I was 1 percent willing, but I needed to be dragged the other 99 percent of the way. I asked Jesus for stability, for a content life, and he showed me the way. He gave me rescue from the true villain that caged me, keeping me from true contentment, and that villain was my gluttony. Jesus can and will bring rescue, and the rescue comes from the wilderness; it's out in the desert, where Jesus is.

Jesus as Our Example of How to Suffer

"Our Savior Jesus Christ." This section of the prayer puts our rescuer front-and-center. His example in times of suffering gives us a trail to follow.

He walked around on our earth experiencing everything we do—hunger, fatigue, and stress; he experienced temptations of all kinds, and yet he did not sin. Because he was tested, we can look to him to know how to withstand our own temptations. Because he suffered, we have an example of how to endure our own suffering. Because he triumphed over death, we can join with him in triumph.

One way to think about fasting is as "chosen suffering." It is a practice in which we allow ourselves to hunger, to lack, to suffer, because we believe there is *good* in it. This isn't a popular view in a world where most people see suffering as something to be avoided at all costs. But there is another way to approach suffering. Jesus chose to die, though it meant great pain, because he knew it was worth the glory to come. Jesus' suffering brought about his ultimate triumph.

Many Christians believe that Jesus suffered so that we don't have to. This is not true. Jesus suffered, and so we will suffer.

> . . . that I may know him and the power of his resurrection, and may share his sufferings, becoming like him in his death, that by any means possible I may attain the resurrection from the dead. (Philippians 3:10–11)

Thinking back to the image of that cushioning layer of fat, I believe we cushion ourselves with pleasures and comforts in order to protect ourselves from lack. Lack isn't bad; it is simply an invitation, a hole asking to be filled. The question is: Do *we* fill it, or do we wait until *Jesus* fills it? Fasting is one way to willingly enter times of lack and allow Jesus to meet us in it.

Jesus' life is our example. By following his example, we are empowered to withstand temptation and even *choose* to enter seasons of lack ourselves in the form of fasting. Jesus demonstrated how to fast and how to suffer well. As I share my own story of lack, I will return again and again to the way Jesus led by example. It was Jesus who best demonstrated how to fast.

Jesus began his ministry with a fast. After John the Baptist baptized Jesus and the Holy Spirit descended on him, our Lord went directly into the wilderness. For the Jews who witnessed Jesus' baptism, a journey into the wilderness was a very familiar thing. The law they practiced reminded them, through feasts, fasts, and traditions, of what they had been saved from (Egypt), what they had been saved through (the wilderness), and what they were saved to (the promised land).

John the Baptist himself lived in the wilderness, fed by God's provision. Through psalms and stories, God's people throughout time have sought to remember the wilderness as the place where one must lean on God for provision, for sustenance—for *life*. Prophets lived in the wilderness, outside of the city where food and shelter were. Prophets depended on God, and they experienced his help on a daily, hourly, even minutely basis.

After their exodus out of Egypt, the Israelites were led into the wilderness, where they would spend forty years living on manna, God's bread from heaven. This story was no doubt in Jesus' mind when he went out into the wilderness and fasted for forty days. Wilderness comes before abundance. The exodus story tells us this; Jesus' temptation in the wilderness tells us this; and the *cross* tells us this. The story of slavery, wilderness, and then abundance runs like a melody throughout the symphony of the Bible and the Christian life. It is a cycle—a rhythm of truth—that brings us continually to the Lord for rescue, provision, and abundance.

Jesus is all three: He is our rescue, he is our manna, and he is our rich reward. We cannot experience the fullness of what he gives us unless we are willing to experience them all. Gluttony robs us of manna. And without first eating manna, we cannot taste the feast. Perpetually feasting prevents us from experiencing hunger—*sitting* in hunger—and letting us look upward to heaven for sustenance. Then, when feasting time comes, we see it for the glory that it is, with wide, unblurry eyes—with tongues not numbed by the constant intake of salty foods, but with pure, unadulterated taste.

Yes, Jesus started his three-year ministry with a forty-day fast. He went out into the desert, and this is what it says in the book of Matthew:

> Then Jesus was led up by the Spirit into the wilderness to be tempted by the devil. And after fasting forty days and forty nights, he was hungry. And the tempter came and said to him, "If you are the Son of God, command these stones to become loaves of bread." But he answered, "It is written, 'Man shall not live by bread alone, but by every word that comes from the mouth of God.'" (Matthew 4:1–4)

Growing up in the church, I have heard this passage preached many times, and every time I heard it preached, the forty days of fasting were described as making the following temptation even more severe. Jesus wasn't just hungry—he had been hungry for forty days! The devil came to him, as most modern preachers would say, at the worst possible time.

During my two-month fast, I dove deeply into what the early church fathers said about fasting. Yes, believe it or not, when one is starving, it is much more encouraging to go read sermons written by those who saw fasting as a treasure and an opportunity. I recall what Lindsay said to me at the time: *Most people pity you, but St. Basil would envy you.* St. Basil the Great taught during a time when asceticism was popular—when Christians inflicted great suffering on themselves, believing it to be a holier way of life.

I am not preaching asceticism. I am not practicing asceticism. I do not believe that suffering is holier than abundance. I do, however, believe that both suffering and abundance have a holy role to play within the Christian life. When a Christian suffers, it is holy; and when a Christian experiences true abundance, it is holy. To be in *Christ*—and to do what he did—is holy!

I want to say that one more time, loud and clear: To be in Christ, and to follow his example, is holy.

The early church fathers taught shortly after the apostles and helped lay the foundations for many church traditions that are still followed today. As I quote them, I am giving honor and weight to Christians and teachers who came before me, not equating them with Scripture but rather giving respect to their excellent teachings.

It is interesting to note and ponder how differently the early church leaders taught about Jesus' temptation in the wilderness compared to how it is taught today. Today, it is commonly taught that the forty-day fast *increased the severity* of the temptation, whereas historically, the early church taught that those forty days *prepared* him for temptation.

This is a significant difference! No *wonder* we don't want to fast! If fasting increases temptation, we should be running to every fast-food drive-through we see, *saving* ourselves from the increased temptation to sin. If fasting increases temptation, then fasting is bad for the Christian. We ask Jesus in the Lord's Prayer, "*Lead us not into temptation.*" Jesus taught us to pray, and he taught us to run from temptation—to seek protection, *deliverance* from it. If fasting increases temptation, it cannot be for our good.

But fasting is good. In his Sermon on the Mount, when Jesus taught about fasting, he said this:

> And when you fast, do not look gloomy like the hypocrites, for they disfigure their faces that their fasting may be seen by others. Truly, I say to you, they have received their reward. But when you fast, anoint your head and wash your face, that your fasting may not be seen by others but by your Father who is in secret. And your Father who sees in secret will reward you. (Matthew 6:16–18)

Jesus does not say, "*If* you fast"; he says, "*When* you fast." Jesus expected his followers to be fasting, not just because it was part of the law, but because it was *good*. Do you notice what it says near the end of this passage? It says, "That your fasting may not be seen by others, but by your Father who is in secret." Fasting is an *intimate* part of our relationship with our Lord. Fasting is a type of prayer that connects us closely to the source of all our needs. Fasting is *good*.

Fasting doesn't increase our temptation, it *prepares* us for it. Think about it: Jesus spent forty days in the wilderness, trusting in the Father for his sustenance. The Bible says that he went to the wilderness *in order to* be tempted by the devil, but what happened first? He fasted. Then, after those forty days, the devil came to him, tempting him with bread. And that was when Jesus spoke the words that I recited *every single day* of my two-month starvation: "Man shall not live by bread alone, but by every word that comes from the mouth of God" (Matthew 4:4).

For forty days, Jesus had been living off the word of God, and he had experienced that it was *enough*. When the devil came to him, presenting him with physical, *tangible* food, Jesus was able to resist, because he had prepared himself. And ultimately, Jesus was preparing for the cross.

I believe that in this story, Jesus gives us an example of how to prepare for temptation. If fasting is a regular part of our lives, whether it is unchosen suffering or chosen fasting, then we are *regularly* being given the chance to experience his sufficiency.

I'll return to gluttony for just a moment. Gluttony is a temptation that is thrown in our faces everywhere we look. Billboards; ads; Netflix; suggested videos on the side bar of our computer screen; Instagram posts; trends; push alerts; coupons in your inbox; FOMO; social events—I could go on and on. The temptation to gorge and binge isn't just presented to us; it is practically shoved into our mouths, and all we have to do is swallow. There is so much richness around us that we have been conditioned by our environment to believe that without these things, and without constant "fullness," we cannot abide.

It's no wonder that fasting seems so abhorrent; it's no wonder we think we need constant "bread" to survive. Without bread—without the tangible comforts and even *necessities* of this world—can we live?

The answer is *yes*: Yes, we can live. We can live, because we don't live by bread alone but by the word of God. It is the word of God—*every* word of God—that keeps us alive. When Jesus was faced with temptation—with bread, with power, with land—he was satisfied with God's word. God's word was *enough* for him. And God's word is enough for us. God's word is what keeps us alive.

I starved for two months, and this was the verse I kept reciting over and over and over again: *Man does not live by bread alone, but by every word that comes from the mouth of God* (Matthew 4:4). When I couldn't swallow the food to keep me alive and when food through a tube didn't seem to satisfy me, God's word and breath kept me alive, and *he* satisfied me.

Fasting gives us the regular experience of God being sufficient for us. The practice of withholding abundance until the proper time strips off the layer of fat that dulls our enjoyment of the world. It forces us to feel both the lack *and* the pleasures. It forces us to turn our eyes toward heaven and beg God for help.

During that two-month stretch, a wise person in my life told me, "Suffering reminds us of how much we always need God." Abundance creates an illusion that we don't need him—it gives us a fantasy world where food, drink, shelter, and safety are sufficient to keep us alive and satisfied. This couldn't be further from the truth. It is God who keeps us alive; it is God who holds the days of our lives perfectly and carefully in his hands; and it is God who gives us what we need, even when we don't ask.

Fasting breaks the illusion of self-sufficiency. Fasting strips back the fat; it tears off the rose-colored glasses; it yanks away the noise-canceling headphones; and it forces us to sit in the quiet, peaceful, *satisfactory* space where it is only God's word keeping us alive. God's word is enough.

I wanted to eat, but I couldn't. I made meals for my family, then hid away while they ate them. I sipped some broth, then spat it up. Then I would sit down, look up at the ceiling, and I would say those words, over and over: *Man does not live by bread alone, but by every word that comes from the mouth of God*. I would sit there and be amazed—amazed at how okay I was. I was hungry; I was empty, and yet I had enough. Part of me wishes I could go back in time and experience those pure, simple moments. The *clarity* I had in the starvation—the assurance that I was going to thrive, even though I couldn't eat, even though I could possibly die. It was the oxymoron of emptiness—emptiness that held perfect satisfaction.

Gluttony makes sure that emptiness is always filled. It is like water flowing downward, filling every crack and space. It must fill *all* lack—the glutton *must* be satisfied *as soon as possible*. Fasting is patient. Fasting is willing to sit in the lack and be curious about how it will be filled. Fasting is the faith in the *true* substance that comes from the mouth of God. Fasting is the discipline that believes that God is enough, and it is the preparation for when temptation comes our way, telling us that he isn't.

As I write this, I am not starving anymore. I have bouts of not eating or drinking, and bouts where I must purge anything I swallow, but I am not starving. I live off liquid, have ways of getting nutrition, and I am no longer starving. I have not experienced anything quite like those two months again, and it wouldn't be healthy for me to *seek* that starvation again. I have a disabled esophagus, and that is a trial I did not, and would not, choose for myself. But because of my suffering, I have an opportunity to experience the true sufficiency that is in Christ.

Those two months were horrifying, but they were also precious. They forced me to cling hard to my Savior, and they prepared me for the temptations that would soon follow. They taught me that Jesus' word was the only thing keeping me alive, and in a sense, it seemed to make me invincible. It was the disrupting, painful, purifying beginning to the hardest year of my life, and I am thankful for it.

Jesus fasted in the wilderness. His fast prepared him for his coming temptation. His fast let him experience how sufficient God's power is while he was weak. Jesus has been my ultimate example. I am able to look at him, what he did, and how he persevered as I endeavored to persevere through my own trials. Jesus was preserved by God in the hardest of times, and this showed me that God would carry me through my own hard times.

Without his example, every attempt at navigating my trial is guesswork. Without him carrying me through, I am left to weather my trials with my own strength. But the Christian's promise in times of suffering is this: Jesus suffered first so we would not have to suffer alone. Suffering need not abandon us to a place of loneliness and defeat. In fact, when we suffer, we are drawn, somehow, closer to Jesus.

3

by bread alone

You have fed us with spiritual food
in the sacrament of his body and blood

After the longest two months of my life, the results were in: My esophagus was dead, and it wasn't coming back. There is nothing to be done for a failed esophagus—nothing to return peristalsis. This struggle to swallow would apparently follow me for the rest of my life and would only get worse. That's when the harder questions started rolling in: Why did this happen? What caused this? What else will it kill? How long do I have?

These questions drove me continually to the creator of my brittle body in desperate prayer: *God, why? Why would you let this happen?* My physical need was great—I was in pain, I was struggling to eat—but my spiritual need was greater. Why would God send me this kind of suffering? What was he *doing*?

My priest came to visit me around this time, and I shared with him how I had been encouraged by Jesus' words, "*Man does not live by bread alone, but by every word that comes from the mouth of God.*" Father Aaron said that he had brought a similar passage to read. In fact, it was the Old Testament passage that Jesus was quoting during his wilderness temptation:

> He humbled you and let you hunger and fed you with manna, which you did not know, nor did your fathers know, that he might make you know that man does not live by bread alone, but man lives by every word that comes from the mouth of the LORD. (Deuteronomy 8:3)

It was such a jarring, startling verse. It read like a slap to the face, a kind, though sharp, stab of reality. It was the *why* behind my trial. *Why* would God allow me to hunger? Could it perhaps be for my good? This was the beginning of my realization that I had been drawing life not from God but from earthly things. I ate for sustenance, yes—but I also ate for pleasure, for fulfillment, and for happiness. Losing those things caused me more suffering than my hungry stomach did, and those things were in want of this lesson: I need the word of the Lord in order to be fulfilled.

It was only the beginning of my diagnostic journey, but one thing was certain: I would not swallow solid food ever again. I imagine that many others who have had to suffer the loss of such a vital bodily function have faced the same sort of paralyzation and inability to metabolize their new reality. Reality had changed, but my mind hadn't accepted it. My throat was permanently disabled, but in my mind, I would still be having steak in the distant future. I could not accept this diagnosis.

Disability, Loss, and Need

My illness causes what is known as an *invisible* disability. Disability isn't a new thing in my family. When I was around fourteen years of age, my father went very suddenly and unexpectedly blind. A rare hereditary disease activated in his eyes, and over the course of a couple years, he went from driving us in cars and reading us books at night to not knowing which of us kids walked into the room until he heard our voices.

He was so quiet and calm about it all that I had no idea what he must have been feeling. He went to all his tests and appointments; he tracked the rate and spread of his blind spots on his computer by inventing his own system; he spoke very matter-of-factly when he explained it to others. But it wasn't until one ordinary day, when I asked for his help installing software on our computer, that I began to comprehend. At that time, he still had a little central vision left, and it made him seem very capable—almost normal. He tried to put the disc into the CD-ROM drive. Several clumsy attempts made him continually drop the disc, until he grunted angrily, dropping the disc with a defeated sigh. After a quiet pause, he said in the smallest of voices, "Will you help me?"

Reality had struck. His blindness hadn't seemed real when he acted as though everything was fine, but it *was* there. He *was* feeling it, and he *was* humbled by it. A capable engineer found himself asking his teenage daughter for help putting a disc into a CPU tower, and that was only the beginning of the sort of things he would need help with in the future. My dad was blind, and it devastated him.

At that time, our family attended a charismatic, evangelical church. We had a loving and supportive community, and one of the ways this care manifested itself was through prayer nights. Groups of us gathered together to pray for healing for my dad's sight. Time after time, we would beg and ask God for healing, and time after time, I would say "amen" with as much confidence as I could muster, then sink into disappointment when my dad remained blind.

There was one prayer night in particular when my dad asked to make an announcement after one of the larger prayer events. He asked the church and those in our community to stop asking for healing. He wanted to embrace his new life. To me, he had given up; to me, he had run out of faith.

That night, I had locked myself in my room, too distressed to come out. I was angry at God and confused about why he had not healed my father's blindness. I was so sure he had become blind only to glorify God through miraculous healing. But after nights of ceaseless prayer, he was still blind. He couldn't see, and his eyesight was not going to come back. I remember Dad knocking softly on my door, asking if he could come in. He sat beside me and listened as I cried and sobbed about how sad I was for him. I wanted his sight restored; I wanted him to walk me down the aisle one day; I wanted him to see me in my wedding dress; I wanted him to be able to see his future grandchildren. Bewildered by the seemingly dismal future ahead with a blind father, I asked him why he was giving up on healing.

I was surprised when the first words that came from his mouth were: "I think you are taking this harder than I am." He thanked me for my compassion and expressed that he didn't think he deserved it. He hugged me and explained to me that he had been on a journey with God, too. He didn't want to pick what a good future for him would be like; he wanted to trust God to decide what a good future was. Dad had asked for healing, and God said "no."

"That can only mean this blindness is good for me," he said. "It will bear fruit, and I want that fruit more than I want healing." Then he said the words that made all my fears, all my questions, and all my anger fall powerless and irrelevant: "I *will* be healed one day. And the next thing I see will be the face of Jesus. That is enough for me."

My dad was fasting. His blindness had created a void of lack in his life, and he wanted to let it be empty so that Jesus could plant seeds and bear fruit inside it. This conversation with my dad formed my theology of Christian suffering. I was so inspired by him; I wanted to be like him. He hadn't run out of faith when he asked for our community to stop gathering to pray for his healing; he had chosen the *harder* faith, the faith that Jesus would be enough in the midst of his blindness.

Dad's faith grew with his blindness; his humility grew. He became a father who delighted in receiving help from his children. He was a husband who spent more time at home. He reached a point where he would at times tell me he was *thankful* for his blindness.

My dad had become aware of what he truly needed. His need for Jesus was greater than his need for sight. While others—at times, including me—may have pitied him, *he* was thankful. He wanted the road God had chosen for him, whatever it was. He wanted spiritual riches more than physical ones.

The week after I received the diagnosis of a failed esophagus, our family went on vacation with my parents. It was a hard, unforgettable vacation. The most likely cause of my failed esophagus was a degenerative and often terminal disease called systemic scleroderma, and the possibility of that diagnosis hung over my head like a death threat. It was a vacation that didn't feel like a vacation: I was barely able to eat enough to stand up straight; I was constantly vomiting or experiencing esophageal blockages; and my head was spinning with endless what-ifs.

I remember coming down the stairs in the vacation house after a phone call with one of my doctors. I sat down beside my dad and sighed. He knew it was me; he knew me by my voice—by my hopeless sigh.

"You're grieving a loss," he said. "I had to do the same with my sight."

I looked up. "A loss?" I hadn't made that connection—that I was like him. Courage rallied within me as he spoke about life with a disability.

"Right now it is time to grieve and be sad," he said, "but a time will come when you come to terms with your new life. I still sometimes wish I could see, but I am at peace with it."

"Would you say you are thankful to Jesus for your blindness and what it did for you?" I asked.

He laughed. "Yes, but not always," he said. "I will always need his help with that."

That was the thing: Whether blind or sighted, my dad needed Jesus. What his blindness did was bring his need for Jesus front and center. It was the same for me: I needed Jesus. I always had, but once I lost food? I desperately felt my need.

Disability, loss, pain, and suffering all create a void inside us. Without sight, there is blindness; without food, there is hunger; without hearing, there is silence; without money, there is poverty; without wellness, there is pain; without safety, there is danger. These voids create need. Need longs to be fulfilled. Need drives us to seek help.

Man cannot live by bread alone, but by every word that comes from the mouth of God.

True life is not to be found simply in our physical needs being met. And when God allows voids to form within our physical wellness, we develop the feeling of urgency.

"I need food! I am hungry!" Those were the urgent cries from my heart. My inability to swallow drove me to cry out to Jesus for food. This is a good and honest cry for help! But God's answer wasn't simply to feed me physical food. What he did was offer me truer help: the bread of his word. His word promised me that life is more than food, and that if I seek after him, he will give me *everything* I need.

> Therefore I tell you, do not be anxious about your life, what you will eat or what you will drink. . . . Is not life more than food? . . . Look at the birds of the air: they neither sow nor reap nor gather into barns, and yet your heavenly Father feeds them. Are you not of

> more value than they? And which of you by being anxious can add a single hour to his span of life? . . . Therefore do not be anxious, saying, "What shall we eat?" or "What shall we drink?" . . . For . . . your heavenly Father knows that you need them all. But seek first the kingdom of God and his righteousness, and all these things will be added to you. (Matthew 6:25–27, 31–33)

That was a monumental vacation with my family. I knew I was going to have to see a doctor for possible systemic scleroderma when I returned home, and that meant facing a potentially terminal disease. A void of need filled me. I didn't just need food to eat—I needed life.

Man does not live by bread alone, but by every word that comes from the mouth of God.

I wanted to live. I needed that "every word" that came from God's mouth. Lindsay and I took a walk together on the last day, talking about the possibility that I might die. I don't distinctly remember all the words said, but I remember it being refreshing to talk plainly about the reality we were in. I remember walking away from that time with one very clear and simple conviction: If I was going to live, it would be because God said I would live.

There was only one prayer left to pray: *Jesus, let me live.*

We went to church shortly after returning home from that vacation. I remember going forward to receive communion. I took the bread and the wine, and I knelt before the altar. I looked down at the cup of port in my hand. I stared at it. I looked at the bread that was too thick for me to swallow. I stared at it.

> I am the bread of life; whoever comes to me shall not hunger, and whoever believes in me shall never thirst. (John 6:35)

> The Word became flesh and dwelt among us. (John 1:14)

> And [Jesus] took bread, and when he had given thanks, he broke it and gave it to [his disciples], saying, "This is my body, which is given for you. Do this in remembrance of me." And likewise the cup after they had eaten, saying, "This cup that is poured out for you is the new covenant in my blood." (Luke 22:19–20)

I drank the wine. I kissed the bread, swallowing a crumb or two. And just like that, I ate the word of God.

Feasting

Fasting and feasting are two extremes on the rotating cycle of contentment in the Christian life. Like winter and summer, both are unique in their beauty and provision. Like the poem in Ecclesiastes 3:2, "*A time to be born, and a time to die; a time to plant, and a time to pluck up what is planted*," there is richness and meaning to be found for the person who experiences contentment and joy in both times of lack and times of abundance.

I want you to think about feasting. What do you imagine? An overflowing table with silver dishes and polished spoons? A roast hog with an apple in its mouth? Full partygoers, leaning back with a groan and loosening their belts? Feasting. Feasting is abundance; feasting is excess; feasting is having *more* than you need to be satisfied. Feasting is good.

Think about what makes your personal experience of Christmas day special. Is it a special food you only eat at Christmas? Is it a heap of presents under a decorated tree? Is it certain family members you only get to see one day a year? This is an example of a feast. It is a time of abundance and celebration—a time when we remember the feast that was given to the earth, Jesus, our Savior—bringing us abundance of life!

Now, think about Good Friday. It is a day when many fast; a day where we sit in silence; a day when we do not shout for joy but rather ponder the cross. This is an example of a fast. Fasting from celebration and excess on Good Friday often makes the feast of Easter that much more exciting!

You can see rhythms of fasting and feasting all throughout Scripture. The Israelites' slavery in Egypt could be symbolic of a fast, and their deliverance through the Red Sea is like a feast. Their forty years in the desert: a fast. The triumphal entrance into the promised land flowing with milk and honey: a feast!

The First Feast

Think back to the garden of Eden. Think about the word "garden": It is a place to find and grow food. The first man and woman were placed in a safe, kept area, with all the food they could ever need, and more than that—they had the Tree of Life. This was the first feast.

> The LORD God took the man and put him in the garden of Eden to work it and keep it. And the LORD God commanded the man, saying, "You may surely eat of every tree in the garden, but of the tree of the knowledge of good and evil you shall not eat, for in the day that you eat of it you shall surely die." (Genesis 2:16–17)

There was life and abundance in the garden, all provided by God. As you can see in this passage, there was both feasting *and* fasting in the garden. Basil the Great called this the first fast: "Fasting is as old as humanity: it was legislated in paradise. It was the first command that Adam received."[1]

Yes, even in the garden, before sin ever came to our world, the Lord God ordained a fast: Do *not* eat from this tree. Man had everything that he needed, and yet, there was something withheld from him.

Eating was introduced to humankind as the promise of life. *Eating* from the Tree of Life meant living forever. *Fasting* from the Tree of the Knowledge of Good and Evil meant avoiding death. This picture in Genesis becomes symbolism that is referenced time and time again in Scripture: eating is associated with life. Humankind ate from the right tree, and they lived; they ate from the wrong tree, and they died.

We must eat food to live. We all know this. But it is not the whole of the truth. I would say that the whole truth is this: We must eat the *right* food to live. From which tree should Adam and Eve eat in order to live? From which tree should they abstain?

When the serpent came to tempt Eve, he told her that God had lied; he told her that God was withholding something good.

> The serpent said to the woman, "You will not surely die. For God knows that when you eat of it your eyes will be opened and you will be like God, knowing good and evil."
>
> So when the woman saw that the tree was good for food, and that it was a sight to the eyes, and that the tree was to be desired to make one wise, she took of its fruit and ate, and she also gave some to her husband who was with her, and he ate. (Genesis 3:4–6)

This was the first temptation of gluttony: *to want more than what God has said is enough*. When Adam and Eve "took" and "ate" from the Tree of Knowledge, they were eating not for life but for something else—something they thought they were missing. Even amid a feast, where there was *more* than what they needed to live, they chose to believe that something was missing.

Feasting is good like the garden of Eden is good. Feasting is enjoying and delighting in God's provision. Gluttony is taking what God has given and then taking more. Gluttony is saying, "The feast isn't enough."

Yes, feasting is good; it is so, so good. And it is not bad to think that we need food to live—not after God our Father showed us in the garden how to eat, saying to humankind, "You may eat anything in the garden." In the same way, when the Israelites were led into the desert after their rescue from Egypt, God sustained them by sending "bread from heaven." And in the same way, Jesus fed the five thousand people who had come to listen to him teach. God has always been a God who feeds his people; he is a God who gives us everything we need. His provision will always be enough.

God-given feasting is the promise of provision—the memory of God's ability to care for and feed his children. Eating is special, and that is why there are meant to be times where the people of God come together and eat food in a celebratory fashion. Whether an Easter feast, a harvest festival, or a Thanksgiving dinner, humankind has associated feasts with times of abundance.

Thinking back to how Adam and Eve "took" and "ate" from the trees in the garden, notice the significance behind Jesus' words to his disciples at the Last Supper: "*Take and eat; this is my body.*"

When Jesus—*our* bread from heaven—came to the earth, he became the new feast. It is his body, the true Tree of Life—it is his blood, pouring like a river of life from his side—that is the real feast. All feasts point to this feast: the Lamb, slain before the foundations of the world (Revelation 13:8). This is the truest feast that the beloved Tree of Life was pointing to; it is the source of the river that flowed through Eden; it is the truest and most abundant meal there is—and in it, we have true, unending life. In it, we have enough.

Take and eat. Christ's body and blood, broken and shed for me—that is my feast. All I need to do is receive it and eat it.

I think back to that moment when I held the bread and the wine in my hands. I wasn't able to swallow physical food, but there *was* a feast for me. There was provision for me. I had the only feast that mattered. I may not have been able to eat a meal, but I could bring the communion bread to my lips with a trusting kiss and taste the wine of Jesus' blood on my tongue. And if I was not able even to do that, I would still have my feast.

Because *man does not live by bread alone, but by every word that comes from the mouth of God.*

The word of God is the bread that gives me life. How can a word be eaten? How can that keep me alive? This is my word: the person and life of Christ. The words from his mouth and the truth of what he has done—these things keep me alive. These things are the true feast, and these things are available to me at any time.

The G-Tube

I held on to that truth as I came to terms with the fact that I would not eat solid food again. Jesus' body could be enough for me, even if I struggled to believe it. He would satisfy me; he *promised* he would satisfy me.

This helped me make the decision to get a gastronomy tube (or "G-tube"). This is a port placed surgically just over the stomach so that I could feed sustenance directly into my stomach, bypassing the esophagus. I had wanted to avoid invasive approaches to nutrition, but once I learned that things would not get much better, we opted for the G-tube so that I wouldn't have to stress about getting enough to eat.

This was supposed to be the end of the hard story—the moment that I could finally get enough to eat. Sure, I didn't get to enjoy steaks and sandwiches, but at least I wouldn't have to be hungry anymore! I could feed myself, sit at the table with my family and syringes, and feel the feeling of fullness.

If only.

The G-tube ended up becoming one of those "out of the frying pan, and into the fire" experiences. A procedure that should have been simple and easy made things so much worse. I will never forget the moment the local anesthesia began to wear off. I couldn't move; I could barely breathe.

I have experienced many different kinds of pain in my life. From screaming in childbirth to vomiting from a traumatic surgery, I thought I had felt it all. This time, I couldn't scream; I couldn't talk; I couldn't move. Tears dripped from my eyes, and I clung to Lindsay's hand as hard as I could.

They kept saying, "This shouldn't be happening; this never happens." They gave me IV pain meds, then again—and again. Nothing got better. I was in so much pain I couldn't stand to use the toilet; I couldn't sit up; I couldn't even tilt my head forward a half inch. I was paralyzed with pain.

For three days in the hospital, they ran tests and tried to figure out what happened. For three days they put nothing into my stomach, and I couldn't eat or drink. Nothing seemed wrong with the tube, but the pain never stopped. The surgeon admitted it had probably been a severed nerve and then sent me home with a bottle of liquid pain meds to inject through the tube.

Sending me home only made things worse. I couldn't swallow, but I also had not been given any training with the tube. After two days of—well, I don't even remember what it was like, because it is still all a dark blur of pain in my mind. But after two days of agony, I sought help from a more experienced and specialized hospital.

By the time they had admitted me there, I was barely coherent. I had dangerously low potassium and extreme dehydration.

Finally, they started me on my tube feeding, and I began to "eat" again. Sadly, the mere presence of food in my stomach was more pain than I could bear. We had it on the slowest drip possible, and still it felt like torture.

I find it hard to write about this. I can't help but think, "Who would even want to read about this?" Recounting the details of that time is like watching a car wreck in slow motion. Who would want to do that? And *why*? I can only assume that you've made it this far into my book because you are willing to hear the story. And while I will do my best to spare you the more agonizing details, I choose to recount my story for this reason: I want you to know how impossible and unbearable the suffering really was for me, so that you can be amazed—like I am—at how *enough* Jesus was, despite my pain. Perhaps it is why we are given details of the crucifixion in the four Gospels. Perhaps knowing just how bad it was makes us marvel over the passage that states: "*For the joy that was set before him* [*Jesus*] *endured the cross*" (Hebrews 12:2).

It is amazing to think that during that time, amid all the pain and hunger, I was somehow able to experience contentment. I had this irrational, incomprehensible enoughness from Jesus, and it sustained me. Perhaps it can't be explained. I was in pain, and he was enough; I had no answers, but he was enough.

I went back and looked at one of my social media posts from the day when I began to receive food from the G-tube. The end of it reads:

> Thank you Jesus—and thank you my friends. I think I'll sleep in peace tonight. Psalm 23 once more comes to my mind as Jesus is with me in the valley, preparing a feast for me in the presence of my enemies. My cup overflows.

That week in the hospital was the emptiest and most helpless I have ever been. And yet, I had my feast. I had the only feast I needed: I had Christ, and he was enough.

It is hard to know what you truly need until you are stripped bare. I have grown up in the West, living a comfortable, middle-class life. I always had food to eat; I had parents who loved me and paid for my college; I had a community to support me throughout my life; I have a husband who cares for me; I have children who are healthy. Yet, with all these things, I chronically feared not having enough. In a life of abundance, I have always been afraid of being in want.

You can imagine how surprising it has been to find myself in situations where I am dying, starving, and in pain, and yet I am still well in the deepest sense of the word. Ironically, as I write this paragraph, I am sitting on a stretcher in an emergency room, receiving IV nutrition during one of my flare-ups. As I sit here, pondering this chapter, I call to mind the words of a hymn:

> Though Satan should buffet, though trials should come
> Let this blest assurance control
> That Christ has regarded my helpless estate
> And hath shed His own blood for my soul
> It is well (it is well)
> With my soul (with my soul)
> It is well, it is well with my soul.[2]

I see these words very differently than I once did. Growing up, I loved this hymn. I heard the words "it is well" as the Christian saying, "Though I suffer, I am okay with it. I am alright." It wasn't until more recently that I realized the true meaning of those words, "It is well with my soul." In this song, the suffering and loss of this world is being contrasted with the wellness of my soul. Though my body is breaking, though trials have come, Christ came and died for me and made my spirit whole. It is well with my soul. My soul is thriving, and my spirit is free. I may experience pain, I know I will struggle to eat, I know I may even die young, but it is well with my soul. My soul is alive and thriving.

Yes, my physical body is fading—decaying from that curse of death brought on by sin. But my soul is hidden in Christ. I will die like Christ, but I will be raised with Christ. Yes: It is well with my soul.

How can one learn contentment? How can we truly experience and believe that Christ is enough both in times of abundance and in times of intense need?

Whether we believe it or feel that we experience it, Christ *is* enough. Sometimes I try to conjure up feelings of positivity, hoping that my determination will provoke contentment. But I don't think that's the answer. Contentment isn't positivity. Back in July 2022, when I was sitting in that hospital room, receiving painful drips of food via my gastronomy tube, I wasn't just "trying to look at the bright side." I was in pain, and I was scared. I was afraid I would never leave that room or go home again. But it was *well with my soul*, and Christ was enough.

There was something remarkably special about that time. I was just a girl in need of food, and I was holding tightly to the cross as if it were all I had. And perhaps it was. I remember Lindsay coming in to visit me at one point. He smiled at me and said, "You look like you're glowing." I felt like it, too. I won't try to rationalize or explain why or how, but Christ sustained me during that time. He was enough.

4

temptation to compensate

Send us now into the world in peace

The G-tube just wasn't working. It was too painful. My care team put together a plan to get me out of the hospital, getting on a pain medication regimen so that I could get the nutrition I needed but also be at home. I wanted the tube removed, but that was easier said than done. Once a gastronomy tube is placed, it cannot be removed until the body has adjusted to its presence, creating an internal tube that leads from the stomach to the outside. If the tube is removed before that tract is formed, then stomach acid can leak into the abdomen, causing an extremely dangerous infection. This meant playing the waiting game.

Finally, I was getting enough to eat through the G-tube! But the pain was so unbearable that it wasn't worth the nutrition. I was in a tough spot, trying to decide what to do. For a month I tried to live a normal life, caring for my four children, taking in nutrition through the tube, and crawling through the pain. I wasn't surviving; I was treading water in an open sea. How long could I last like that?

During that time, Lindsay had a work trip to attend out of town. He was only gone for a day before I called him back. I remember feeling so guilty having to ask him to drive home in the middle of his trip, only to summon an ambulance to take me back to the hospital. At our wits' end, we begged the emergency room staff to remove the tube. I didn't care if it meant not eating—I just wanted it out! I described the feeling as an arrow piercing my organ, causing me endless torture. The doctors said they could not in good conscience take it out yet, not without risking infection.

I became desperate. I needed to be free. I assured the doctors I could get enough nutrition by mouth if they would just take it out. So they gave me a week to try and drink fluids through my esophagus. If I could live off a liquid diet, they would see if they could remove it once it was safe to do so.

I worked really hard to get nutrition through my mouth alone. Thankfully, that month of receiving nutrition through the G-tube had given my swollen esophagus enough of a rest. I found it easier to get clear liquids through. Then finally, after what felt like an eternity, the doctor removed the gastronomy tube.

It was as if a switch had been flipped. I came off the narcotics, I threw out all of my formula bottles, and I zoomed back into my old life. I wanted those horrible months behind me, and I wanted to feel *normal* again. Sure, my stomach was still in pain from the severed nerve, but it was *nothing* like what it had been before. I was free! Or so I thought.

That sick Tasha who had posted updates and asked for prayer on social media dropped off the map, and the old, "free" Tasha came back. Sure, I was still condemned to a life on a liquid diet, but at least I wasn't eating out of a tube anymore! At least I wasn't on narcotics, and I could drive! At least I wasn't needing to rely on other people, and I could take care of my family. I couldn't swallow the food I was making, but I could cook fancy meals again for *other* people! I could taste the food and spit it out.

In my mind, the fast was *over*. I didn't *want* to fast anymore. I wanted to feast. I wanted life. I wanted excess. I was so tired of experiencing lack and sitting in the intensity of pain. I was ready for comfort again, and I was going to find it, one way or another.

It was the post-fast gorge. The "*I am so glad that's over and done with*" flip-flop. I did my hard thing, and now I got to make up for all that lack with a whole bunch of self-pampering.

I want to pause here. I want to pause in order to make something very clear: Before I go on and talk about the Tasha who "coped," the Tasha who "gorged," or the Tasha who "hid," I want to say that I am very proud of and thankful for that Tasha. I am thankful for the woman who walked that road, only to fall into a pit—because she did eventually climb out again. She did fight for more, and when she hid and indulged, it was because she was scared and traumatized.

Everyone's story is different. Everyone's times of suffering are speckled with ups and downs, regrets and rewards. The Tasha that I am going to describe in this chapter is *me*. It is me every single day of my life. It is not that I am no longer someone who wants to hide and numb my various trials; I simply have a framework for how to talk to and lead her.

Friend, I am so scared. I am scared of being in pain; I am scared of dying; I am scared of feeding tubes; I am scared of sadness; I am scared of feeling alone; I am scared of what I am going through; and I am constantly scared that this trial will continue through the rest of my life.

If you are someone who feels drawn to shame-filled thoughts when you are weak, then I want you to hear these words: I am not writing this chapter in order to shame myself or any others who have tried to relieve their pain. I am writing this chapter to the scared and weak parts of us, holding out a hand to say, "Don't be afraid; it is safe to come out."

Send us now into the world in peace.

That is the line of the prayer for this chapter. Send us now into the world in *peace*. "Peace" is the word I return to again and again. This next stage of my journey is about the temptation—the impossibly forceful *desperation*—to compensate for the emptiness and lack created by my suffering. I had been sent back into the world, and I did not have peace. I did not have that contentment of "a weaned child with its mother" (Psalm 131:2). I had an unquenchable thirst for comfort. I needed to fill that tiresome void of hunger.

Friend, I was so tired of not eating. I wanted the "Three T's" again! The Three T's is what I call the things I missed the most about eating solid food: taste, temperature, and texture. I wanted to feel happy and full again. I wanted to experience the euphoria of abundance and feasting!

Sure, I couldn't feast on solid food, but I could find ways to feast in *other* ways. I launched headfirst into enjoying myself. If I had to live on a liquid diet, then why not enjoy it? My inability to eat solid food created a void of hunger and longing, and alcohol was the first thing to fill that void. Yes, it filled the void, numbing my mind, my heart, my judgment, and even my pain. The alcohol momentarily took away the feeling of lack and gave me a dose of feasting happiness. Alcohol could be my pet pleasure, I thought. I wouldn't let it get out of control; I simply needed my own treat. When Lindsay and the kids ordered pizza, I could make myself a Rusty Nail. When other people ordered fancy meals at the restaurant, I could order a Cosmopolitan. There—problem solved!

Before I knew it, I wasn't really fasting anymore. Sure, I wasn't eating solid food, but I was still finding abundance from other sources. I hated the lack; I was tired of the lack—tired of the manna. I wanted *more.*

Gluttony—The Drunkenness of Food

My struggle with alcohol makes for an ideal metaphor. Alcohol numbs. It dulls sensitivity to sadness, happiness, pain, hunger, other people's pain, needs, and so much more. It acts as a separation, like a layer of protective fat around the heart and mind, shielding its victim with its pleasurable glaze of anonymity. There are times and places for this kind of drink, consumed in moderation, but I am specifically focusing on what happens when alcohol is used as a cure or an escape from unhappy feelings.

When you turn to alcohol for this reason, you go on an unsuccessful journey toward relief. As I said, alcohol numbs—and the more you partake, the more you think it will help you, and the more miserable you become. If you have consumed enough, you feel the freedom and bliss of drunkenness. You are no longer a person with judgment and clarity; you are a spirit, led here and there by the whims of your inebriated impulses.

In my experience, drunkenness gives the illusion of weightlessness. It provides a mirage of safety and shelter from the storms and deserts of trial. Drunkenness is the result of excess without contentment. It happens when we are not consuming pleasures in order to be at peace but to be *euphoric*.

Euphoria is the anticipated result of gluttony but never the actual result. A moment of euphoria promises to last forever but is over as quickly and easily as it came. It is impossible for the glutton to *ever* be full enough to be satisfied. I mean, really—this is why there was such a place as a "vomitorium" in the Roman Empire. Gluttonous feasts in those times involved vomiting once full, in order to eat *more* food! And for me, it didn't matter how many times I woke up with a hangover headache or apologized for stupid things I had said or done while under the influence of liquor, the next day I would still chase that feeling of euphoria that I was *sure* I had experienced the night before.

My pain and hunger created a lack. That lack longed to be filled. And not only did I want that lack filled, I wanted it overflowing. I didn't just want to be at peace; I wanted euphoria.

> I have learned, in whatever situation I am, to be content. I know how to be brought low, and I know how to abound. In any and every circumstance, I have learned the secret of facing plenty and hunger, abundance and need. I can do all things through him who strengthens me. (Philippians 4:11–13)

I love this passage. The apostle Paul writes here about true contentment. I have always been drawn to this passage, appreciating the nuance of finding contentment in both times of plenty and times of lack. Much conversation around contentment involves learning to be satisfied during times of lack, but I believe that it is just as hard—if not harder—to be content during times of abundance. The discontented feaster stares at their plate full of food and sighs, wondering what *more* they might need to be satisfied.

Drunkenness is a problem of contentment in times of plenty (see Philippians 4). The drunkard consumes more than they actually need, thinking that more is better—that euphoria is just one more drink away. And whether or not the drunkard achieves that feeling of euphoria, it is never a lasting thing. Euphoria isn't *actual* peace or contentment; it is a momentary and fleeting *feeling*.

Peace isn't merely a feeling. True peace is being content with what God has given, no matter the circumstances. Being at peace is to be like a weaned child, sitting beside its mother, enjoying her company. Being at peace is for that child to be free to ask for something, yet also free to *not* ask, knowing and trusting that all its needs are fulfilled.

Yes, in my drinking I chased euphoria, and I also chased the feeling of numbness. To be numb is to feel nothing, to simulate nonexistence. It is to be a bodiless spirit, observing rather than partaking in the surrounding world. Numbness allows a person to be free of not only pain but of joy and other experiences that can result in disappointment. Numbness is desirable for those who have experienced trauma and pain, whether physical, mental, emotional, or spiritual. Numbness is the promise of relief from that pain. Unlike euphoria, which is the *feeling* of rightness in the body, numbness is the *absence* of feeling anything. Numbness is relief from having a body at all.

Euphoria focuses too much on the body, promising that relief can be found by feeling the right feelings inside one's flesh, whereas numbness pulls the focus away from the body altogether, promising that relief can be found outside of the flesh. To put it simply, euphoria pulls us inside ourselves, and numbness pushes us outside of ourselves: to be body-obsessed, or to be bodiless.

We all feel the need to find relief from our suffering. I felt this need; I felt it to the point of desperation. Alcohol offered me the promise of these two things: euphoria and numbness. I would take either one if they gave me the illusion of relief. Alcohol promised me relief through the pampering of my body through its pleasurable taste, and it promised me relief through *freedom* from my pain-ridden body through drunkenness.

I began to drink daily. The self-sabotaging schemer inside of me put rules and boundaries around my drinking, making me believe that I didn't have a problem. I never actually got drunk (at least, that is what I told myself); I never exceeded two drinks (at least, not unless someone else left an unfinished drink on the table); and I never had a drink without telling Lindsay (well, unless I found just cause for having another while he was out of the house).

Alcoholic consumption wasn't the only form my denial took. I found other ways to try and feast. Triggered by moments of FOMO, I would do anything to avoid the fast I was in. Sure, I couldn't swallow, but I could spend money; I could order expensive, fancy soups; I could binge-watch television shows—and I could even try and swallow food that I knew would cause me esophageal blockages.

I wasn't in a stage of careless *sin* or defiant *rebellion*—though sin did have its place in my heart. I was a sufferer, trying to self-soothe and ease the intensity of my trial. It is human to seek to be free of pain and isolation, and it is not sinful to wish to be free of one's allotted trial. If it were, then Jesus would have been in sin for asking God, "Please take this cup from me," just before he faced the cross. But looking to Jesus as an example, he finished that prayer with the words, "Not my will, but yours, be done" (Luke 22:42).

I don't think that, as Christians, we should choose maximum pain and suffering when given the opportunity. Much of my journey has involved seeking out healthy ways of treating pain. But I do think there is something to be said for choosing sober-mindedness when faced with trial. (We will unpack this more in the following chapter.)

Right now, I want to return to the word peace. I think of peace as sitting in contentment, *allowing what God has given to be enough*. As I push gently back on my stage of trying to fill the void of my hunger, I want to be clear about what I am *not* pushing back on.

I am not saying that a Christian should refuse pain relief or comfort.

I am not saying that trials are the most effective when they are most painful.

I am not saying Christians should sit in lack simply to suffer *more*.

I am not saying Christians shouldn't seek out enjoyable experiences to alleviate the intensity of their suffering.

I am not saying that alcohol is bad.

I am not saying that feasting is bad!

Here is what I *am* saying: True relief comes not from numbing or euphoria, but from peace—*true* peace, the peace of Christ, and what he has given.

The Peace of Allowing What God Has Given to Be Enough

If the ultimate relief is peace, then I shouldn't *need* alcohol, binging, numbing, or vice. Peace is possible without those things. In fact, it is a free gift. Peace is accessible if I would only sit quietly and patiently, like Mary sat at Jesus' feet, long enough to realize it is something Christ has already given. The peace of Christ is always there, always ready, always enough.

I was so scared of reliving the trauma and discomfort I had experienced—scared it would become the rest of my life. Even though I had been sustained and at peace while I had the G-tube, I was *tired* of trying so hard. I was tired of manna and tired of God's supernaturally sufficient presence. At the first chance of my old normalcy, I lunged at whatever habits and activities made me feel like my old self.

Suffering, lack, and trial create voids of emptiness, and I *hate* emptiness. I want to be full; I need to be full. The inability to swallow made my greatest fear the center of my world; I was forced to face a life of unending lack. Hunger would flavor the rest of my life, and that terrified me.

This frightened Tasha had a strong idea of what comfort and ease would look like with such a prognosis. This idea of comfort was echoed and encouraged by the sympathetic voices around me, and whether they originated from inside me or outside of me, they said this: *What's happening to you is horrible. You shouldn't have to go through this. The emptiness you feel isn't good. Try filling that need with other things so that you may suffer less. Do everything you can to fill or avoid the emptiness. Seek happiness and comfort, and it will ease your suffering.*

This message comes from the lips of kind-hearted and well-meaning people. It comes from people in my life who are pained to see me suffer. This message also comes from the lips of those who believe that suffering is ultimately bad and should be avoided at all costs.

It is my belief that suffering has a holy role to play in the Christian life. The suffering that Christ experienced on the cross brought abundance to not only himself but the entire world. The gift of *us* and the desire to please his Father was enough for Jesus to endure his trial. And in holding tightly to this truth, we can more boldly respond with obedience to Christ when he compels us to "take up our cross and follow him." It was Saint Isaac the Syrian who said, "Without tasting of Christ's sufferings with understanding of their significance, the soul will never be in communion with him."[1]

My suffering may look scary, and my emptiness might seem cruel. But my emptiness is not cruel or evil; my emptiness is good. My emptiness is good like the empty tomb is good.

If I did not experience this emptiness inside myself, I could never have experienced the miracle of how Jesus chose to fill it. If I had not put down the whiskey bottle, taken off the headphones, or sat inside the silence of my lack, I might never have heard the voice of my Savior—I might never have received the true riches that could only be given through this particular trial.

Like Paul, whose weakness was allowed so that the strength of Christ could be demonstrated, my hunger has allowed something beautiful and profound to be made manifest. There is something good that could only have happened if I had experienced this trial. As Saint Gregory of Nazianzus, one of the early church fathers, once said, "I don't consider it good that you . . . should agonize over your suffering as if it were incurable and irredeemable. Rather, I should want you to be philosophical about your suffering and show yourself superior to the cause of your affliction, beholding in the illness a superior way towards what is ultimately good for you."[2]

This trial has resulted in a simple, quiet testimony from my lips. It sounds something like this: "I am empty, but Christ is enough."

This testimony can't come from a Tasha who has filled her emptiness with drink or distraction. This testimony can only come from a Tasha who has finally chosen to sit in her lack and accept it.

The Tasha sitting in this emptiness is scared. She is hungry. She is in pain. You may be tempted to say sweet and kind words to that Tasha, words like: *This shouldn't be happening to you! You shouldn't have to go through this!*

Those are kind things to say. I always choose to receive words like those as kindness. But Jesus' intentions for me are not just to heal the brokenness of my physical body. He wants to heal the brokenness in my soul. In allowing sickness and pain in my life, Jesus is alerting me to a deeper work that needs to be done in me. John Chrysostom, another of the early church fathers, so beautifully articulated this nuance of suffering: "Ordinarily we experience no pain when the soul is sick, yet on the contrary when the body is troubled we use every means possible to relieve that trouble. For this very reason God afflicts the body because of the sins of the soul, in order to restore health to man's most noble aspect by making the use of the least noble affliction."[3]

I have been told that physical pain is good because it is my brain's system for alerting me that something is wrong. When I feel pain in my ankle after twisting it, it pushes me to ice it. When I have a headache, I am reminded to drink water. Pain helps me care for the brokenness in my body. What John Chrysostom explains is how physical affliction is often the way God alerts us to the fact that there is important work to be done in the soul. It shifts our focus, causing us to cry out to him for help.

Chrysostom also said: "The physician is not only a physician when he orders baths, adequate nourishment, and when he orders the patient to walk through flower gardens, but also when he burns and cuts. . . . Thus, knowing that God loves us more than all the physicians combined, we need not worry nor have any need to ask him to justify the means he employs. Rather, whether he wants to be indulgent or severe, let us abandon ourselves to him. For by either of these means, his desire is always to save us and to unite us to himself."[4]

Oh, how I am floored as I read those words, *Let us abandon ourselves to him*. This is something you can only do with someone you trust. "Not my will but your will be done": That is what we must say to our Physician, who cares more for us than any earthly person. This is what I must do in order to survive this time of physical trial: I must throw myself to Jesus with reckless abandon, trusting that—and here are those final words from the quote that bring me to tears as I read them—*his desire is always to save us and to unite us to himself.*

Oh, dear brothers and sisters in Christ who feel compelled to comfort me with the words, *This shouldn't be happening to you! You shouldn't have to go through this!* Such words drive me to temporary forms of relief that promise to take away the pain and sadness—things like alcohol. Those words are not strong enough to comfort me. I need true comfort. I need to know there is intentionality and purpose behind my suffering.

After going through that first year of hunger and emptiness, here is what *I* think that scared, weary, and comfort-desperate Tasha needed to hear:

Jesus is still enough. I know the pain is hard, but that will not change simply because you want it to change. That drink that sounds so satisfying right now will grant you a moment of placebo relief and then sink you into further misery. It is a lie—a wolf hidden in sheep's innocent clothing—masquerading as your Savior. I have nothing but shame and disappointment in store for you. You are in pain, and that makes you want to vacate your broken body. You are hungry, and that makes you want to fill your body with every kind of fullness and pleasure. Hunger and pain will come and go the rest of your life, and there is no escape from being a soul in a body. There is, however, true peace for that soul and body. There is peace that is sufficient when you are hungry and in pain, and peace that is sufficient when you are full and happy.

True peace is a person. This person is with you. He will raise your body from the dead; he will feed you with enriching food; he will never leave you alone; he will use this pain and hunger to transform your soul; and his presence will make every single moment of your life not only bearable but beautiful.

He has plans and purpose for every moment that you are hurting. He will only allow the pain and the hunger to last a set amount of time. That suffering will produce good things inside you, and it will be worth it.

You do not need to find this peace by looking. You do not need to comprehend this peace in order to enter into it. It is so accessible and so attainable that a child could find and receive it. This peace isn't a revelation or a goal—it is simply there. It is a gift. Receive it. Receive it, and you will be satisfied. This peace is the presence and person of Christ.

Like a wife who is simply *there*, when all her distracted husband has to do is turn off his gaming console to speak with her, or like a salad that is simply *there*, and all the glutton has to do is push away the distraction of the burger in order to see it as desirable, or like beautiful scenes of nature that are *there*, if you would only walk outside your door—healing silence is *there*, and all you need to do is take off your headphones.

Peace is possible. When food, noise, comfort, distraction—or any other thing that might steal our primary attention—have been set aside, a vacancy opens. It is a vacancy waiting to be filled. Our culture has provided us with countless ways of filling in this vacancy and expects that we will always seek to be full. I remember several years ago, when I was trying to lose weight for my health, a friend gave me some advice: "*If you stop feeling scared or threatened by the sensation of hunger, everything will change. Hunger* isn't *bad, and it doesn't always need to be fulfilled.*" I was both fascinated by and terrified of this idea. I had always treated hunger as a purely negative sensation. How paradigm-shifting it was to realize that most humans throughout time had learned to live with the sensation of hunger, and yet here I was, thinking that it was torture!

This inability to tolerate hunger or emptiness is an inability to find peace in all circumstances. When we struggle to find peace in the midst of hunger or even pain, we are attaching qualifying factors to the idea of peace. We are saying that peace is only attainable if *x, y, z*. No wonder I become terrified at the sensation of emptiness: that emptiness will steal my peace from me!

Mercifully, this is not true. Peace is possible both in times of hunger and in times of fullness.

The Peace of Christ

Peace is the promise from heaven, the remedy to the curse. Peace is the gift that satisfies the soul, no matter our circumstances. Peace is the relief from the hurt of all forms of pain. Peace is the shield from the brokenness of humanity.

When the pleasures of this world promise you that euphoria will bring you relief from the sadness of your loss, Jesus promises peace; and when the vices of this world promise you that numbness will bring you relief from the pain of your suffering, Jesus promises peace.

This is not a peace that is momentary or trivial. It is not like silence after a disturbingly loud song or calm waters after a turbulent typhoon. It is not a peace that comes and goes. It is the peace that can calm your ears during that loud song, or the peace that carries you gently through the turbulent typhoon.

The peace of Christ is profoundly steady. It does not waver or change; it is constant. It is not accessible only by *feeling* or *detecting* it; it is given. Whether you feel euphoric or numb, it is available to you; whether you are in pain or not, it is available to you; and whether you are sad, depressed, angry, or hopeless—it is still there, still the same, and still waiting for you. Regardless of your feelings, your bodily state, or your mental health, the peace of Christ is there.

Euphoria is simulated stability, a fleeting feeling of rightness. It promises peace in the moment only to abandon you cruelly, much sooner than you had anticipated. It leaves you thirsty with an urgency to chase it, if only just for one more sip of its intoxicating happiness. But peace is not just an emotion to be felt or a goal to achieve. It is not the feeling of rightness; it is the reality of rightness. Peace is the truth that you have enough, and it is a truth that is yours to grasp.

Where euphoria is a vapor, slithering away through your fingers as you try to grasp it, peace is a foothold on a mountainside or a railing on a swinging bridge. It is the presence of actual support—a firm, reliable reality to clutch. It will hold you up and keep you from falling because it is real, and it isn't going anywhere. All you need to do is reach out and grasp it.

Now, I realize it might sound simple to say, "The peace of Christ is there; all you need to do is receive it!" But if you are anything like me, whenever you are trying to tackle and understand something new, you want a road map. *Sure*, you may say, *I need to receive the peace of Christ—but how? What am I supposed to do?*

I would answer that question in two parts. First, the peace of Christ is found right where you are; and second, the peace of Christ is found in his word.

The Peace of Christ Is with You

"Peace be with you" is something the people of Christ have learned to say to one another. It was the greeting used by Christ to his followers, a greeting not uncommon to the people of Israel. I'll risk sounding cliché by saying this: If peace is a person, and that person is Christ, and Christ is with you, then *peace is always with you*. And I will risk sounding snappy, too: If you cannot find peace, and the person of Christ is with you, *then where are you?*

You are not in the present.

Think about that empty void made by your suffering. Think about what you tend to fill it with. What is the noise that fills your silence? What is the comfort that cushions your sadness?

Jesus is with you, offering the peace of his presence, but when you plug your ears and cover your eyes, you might find comfort in the escape from your emptiness, but you deprive yourself of the peace that is offered to you at every moment. Jesus is present in each moment of your life. If you refuse sobriety in the face of your pain, you miss out on the true rescue from it. If you would just take off the headphones, you might hear his voice; if you would just open your eyes, you might see his face.

If you are struggling to connect with his profound peace, then I ask you this: Are you really allowing yourself to be present in the midst of your trial? Are you willing to do this with your eyes open?

Jesus is with you at all times. When you make space for him and you enter into his presence, he will be enough.

The Peace of Christ Is Found in His Word

When Jesus took the form of a human and visited us on this earth, a miracle happened. The Gospel of John explains it in a unique way: "*The* Word *of God became flesh*," it says. Hundreds of books have been written trying to explain this sentence. That's not surprising—it's a very odd statement. How does a word become a person?

The fantasy author in me wants to answer that question with a healthy dose of symbolism and imagery. How does a word become a person? Well, how was the physical world made way back in the beginning? God spoke, and it came to be. "The Word became flesh." Here is how I will interpret that phrase: *The God who spoke you into flesh has become flesh himself.*

The word of God is alive, and it is potent. The Word *is* God; it is what he did and what he does; it is his character; it is his words; it is the life he lived on the earth—it is his story. The word of God is with you, it brings you peace, and the word of God *changes* you.

When you open your Bible and read the words written within, you are not just interacting with words, no—the word of God is *happening to you*. As your eyes study the words and your mind begins to understand, the Word changes and transforms you.

Yes, the word of God *happens* to you.

When you hear the Bible read from the pulpit on Sunday morning, your mind and heart are transformed by the Word. When you recite and memorize Scripture, or meditate on his word, your character is shaped by it. When you believe in his Word and proclaim it through the waters of baptism, you are adopted into a new eternal family. When you take communion into your hands and eat the Word of God, it is like eating from the very Tree of Life.

Yes, the word of God is like a seed. If you plant it inside you—letting it grow roots into your soul, gain height through your maturation, and bear fruit in your life—it will change you forever.

When the Word is with you, peace is with you. When you are willing to remain in the void made by your suffering, you are given the opportunity to be changed by God's Word. Like I said earlier, Jesus is always in the present. He is present with you in his word. If you allow yourself to be present in your lack and sadness, his peace will find you, and you *will* be changed.

How I Have Found Peace in His Word

I write this chapter from a hospital gurney. I have been in here for nearly a full week now, fighting pain and hunger with IV medicine and nutrition. My mind is altered cruelly by the pain medications, and I find it hard to put even two words together or to even know if what I am writing makes sense.

Sometimes I don't *feel* the peace that is mine; I just have to remind myself that it is there. Jesus is present with me. In moments like these, when I am in pain and confused, alone in a hospital room, away from my family, I crave the *feeling* of peace. What I need is *true* peace. I need something bigger than a feeling. I need something bigger than what can be felt and experienced inside of myself.

This is what I love about the peace of Christ: It is so much bigger than me. Like staring at the horizon, knowing the world is too vast to be seen all at once, God's peace is so boundless that

I cannot see where it begins and ends. His love is so profound, I can only understand it in small parts, shown to me in new ways every single day. The truth of his word is so true that I cannot hope to understand it all. I do not *need* to understand it all; I simply need to accept it as truth. I need the truth of his word spoken to me—*given* to me—so that the only part I need to play is to accept it and cherish it.

I don't need to be a theologian to understand and receive the word of God. Jesus says that one must be like a child to enter his kingdom (Matthew 18:2–5). A child doesn't try to understand everything; a child simply accepts that the world is big, and they accept how small they are.

Receiving the peace of God's word for me has been like a child sitting on the lap of their mother, listening to her kind and loving words. In my weakness and fragility, this is how I have endeavored to receive his peace: I have listened to his words.

Man does not live by bread alone, but by every word that comes from the mouth of God.

I know it might sound old-fashioned or rote to say that reciting Bible verses is the answer. But all I can tell you is my own story and how it was that I found comfort and true peace in a life that felt as though everything was being taken away.

Saying words out loud changes you. And saying living, holy, powerful words out loud doesn't just *change* you; it *transforms* you. The God whose words brought an entire world and countless souls to life is the same God who spoke the words in his Holy Scripture. Saying those words has changed me.

I have woven Scripture into my daily life as a result of my chronic pain and hunger, and it has helped me connect physically to the spiritual truth that I am okay. Our family prays Scriptures together each morning and evening. I designed myself a prayer bracelet that helps me return to Scripture when I am scared. I have begun to design and print biblical artwork to help me reflect more on the story of Jesus' life. These things have been more satisfying and sustainable than my vices have ever been.

The truth of God's word can be experienced in so many ways. The logical mind can dig into theology; the lover of beauty can indulge in the poetry of Proverbs; the passionate musician can sing through the Psalms—the Word of God is alive, and he is with us. If we would only enter into that sacred space of the present where he resides, there are infinite ways of being amazed and fulfilled by him.

I did finally choose to give up alcohol and other forms of seemingly benign distractions. I laugh aloud with myself as I reflect on how inspired and alive I felt in the season that followed. You can laugh with me too: between September 2022 and March 2023, I wrote an epic fantasy trilogy, all focusing on the symbolism of the body, suffering, and contentment. Whether sitting in my armchair with a heat pack on my wounds or hooked up to an IV in the hospital, my fingers caught fire with movement as I typed away. Whether or not that trilogy ever sees the light of day, this is still true: I have never been more inspired, more fruitful, or more content than when I am allowing myself to be fueled by my suffering rather than ruled by it.

During my current hospital stay, I was serenaded by a harpist who visits the patients here. When she played for me, I sat back and closed my eyes, listening to the melodies. The music she played cut through the noise of my pain and confusion like a knife. It penetrated my heart and brought a sort of relief to my soul that I didn't know was possible. My body was in pain, my mind was confused, and my stomach was hungry, but the music bypassed all of those things, and I found myself able to dwell solely on the beauty of the music. It did something to me; it changed me.

This is what the word of God is like in our suffering. It speaks to our souls as if in another language, and it changes us. Suffering that had seemed to be unbearable became small, and questions which seemed to torment my mind had been nullified.

The Word of God—this soul-penetrating music—is what keeps us alive. He speaks life and truth into our hearts, showing us just how real he really is.

Choosing the Fast

There are two ways of surviving a season of lack. We can either resist it, stuffing our stomachs with whatever we have access to, or we can choose it, calling it a "fast." Choosing the fast is a prayer. It is a mindset that chooses to sit in our times of emptiness, believing that there are special riches to be found only inside that emptiness at that time. What if a trial wasn't just something to be endured? What if a trial was an *opportunity*?

That trilogy I wrote could have only been written at that time, in that trial. I am so thankful for those days now. I don't feel the pain or hunger I felt back then in those moments—I only feel the joy of what I created. This is what contentment gives us: It gives us more than enough.

Don't think of lack as meaningless emptiness; think of lack as a hole dug out to plant a seed. Every moment of suffering and trial you face has a space for a unique seed. Plant that seed, and invest in your pain. Invest in your trial. Plant every seed at every opportunity. Because I promise you: Any seed planted in the fertile soil of God's perfect presence *will* grow, *will* flower, and *will* yield you a harvest you could never have anticipated.

5

staying awake

Grant us strength and courage to love and serve you

I was hungry. I was in pain. And I chose to actually feel those things by not turning to numbing, vice, or gluttony to rescue me. It seemed so inspiring and exhilarating to *do the hard thing!* Alas, facing the pain and hunger was like facing my own cross: worth it in the end, though incomprehensibly costly. I needed strength and courage to face my situation and to let it do a refining work in me.

This became a long stretch of time where I went through waves of acceptance, alternated with waves of denial. For a time, I would hold on to the fast and let Jesus be enough. I would seek him, pray, worship, and even delight in the beauty of my closeness with my Lord. Then my feelings would change for a time. I would grow complacent and try to hide. I would find ways to convince myself I could avoid how hard it was to be me, and I would struggle to have the faith to keep going.

Here is something I love about serving our Lord Jesus Christ: He says, "My yoke is easy, and my burden is light" (Matthew 11:30), and, "[I] will not let you be tempted beyond your ability" (1 Corinthians 10:13). He does ask us to "pick up our cross" (Matthew 16:24–26), but like Simon of Cyrene, who came to help carry Jesus' cross on the road to Calvary (Matthew 27:32), Jesus promises that we are not alone during the hardest of times. *He* did the hard work of dying on the cross, and we get to taste a portion of that suffering when he allows us to walk through times of trial.

In this chapter, when I talk about facing hardships and allowing trials to do refining work in us, I am *not* saying that you should increase your suffering in order to be more godly. It is not a bad thing to seek to be free of pain. It is not a bad thing to seek comfort, sympathy, help, or healing. Of *course* we must do this! Our Father tells us to ask him to fulfill our needs, and he will *only* allow the suffering that has been given to us as a refining gift—it is a way to be like Christ that is truly beautiful if we hold on to him for the strength and courage we need to weather it.

Alas, there are ways to hide from our trials and let them pass us by in the most tolerable way possible rather than allowing them to do a refining work in us. As followers of Christ and walkers of the way of the cross, we know that God has ordained good works and also hardships for us to walk through. Like a parent who allows their child to join a sports team where there will be a lot of hard work, God has only allowed hardships that can better us and transform us to be more like himself. And in order to reap these rewards, we must face the forces that come against us, empowered by *strength* and *courage* that are granted to us by the Holy Spirit.

It is important to identify which burdens or hardships we are meant to **cast onto the Lord**, which we are meant to **seek freedom from**, and which we are meant to **carry for a time**. For myself, I needed to cast my mortality, my lack, and my fears on God. I needed to seek freedom from pain and starvation—and that meant seeing many doctors and going through all the diagnostic tests and so on. And as far as what I needed to carry for a time? I needed to be the girl who couldn't eat food. I needed to be the girl who suffers from intermittent pain—pain that cannot always be taken away.

It is the burdens that we are meant to **carry for a time** that we need strength and courage to face. It is these burdens that we can either face head on, riding them like waves in the ocean, or we can resist them, allowing ourselves to be tumbled over and half-drowned by the waves. In the stretch of time that followed, I did both. Sometimes I stayed awake—facing my condition with courage and pressing in to try to embrace the trial God had given me. And sometimes I fell asleep—overwhelmed and dismayed by my lot and hiding away, pretending it wasn't happening.

To put it simply, "staying awake" means choosing faith and hope in God, actively holding on to him in times of trial. "Falling asleep" is what we do when we lose sight of Jesus, slipping into a place of fear and denial.

Grant us strength and courage to love and serve you—in both good times and hard times, we need strength and courage. We need the strength to endure this mortal life, and we need courage to face it with eyes wide open. Our desire is to *love* and *serve* our Lord, and even when we walk through the valley of the shadow of death, we have opportunities to love and serve him, provided we stay vigilant and watchful.

A couple of parables will illustrate this point. In Matthew 25, Jesus is explaining to his disciples what the kingdom of heaven will be like. In these parables, he is describing what it will be like to be God's people once Jesus has ascended into heaven. With his Spirit living inside those who believe him, the invisible kingdom of heaven is growing and thriving in the body called the church.

The parable of the ten virgins illustrates the importance of vigilance in God's people. If we are not watchful, we will miss the blessing we have waited and worked so hard for—and in the case of this parable, it is the Bridegroom, Jesus himself.

> The kingdom of heaven will be like ten virgins who took their lamps and went to meet the bridegroom. Five of them were foolish, and five were wise. For when the foolish took their lamps, they took no oil with them, but the wise took flasks of oil with their

> lamps. As the bridegroom was delayed, they all became drowsy and slept. But at midnight there was a cry, "Here is the bridegroom! Come out to meet him." Then all those virgins rose and trimmed their lamps.
>
> And the foolish said to the wise, "Give us some of your oil, for our lamps are going out." But the wise answered, saying, "Since there will not be enough for us and for you, go rather to the dealers and buy for yourselves." And while they were going to buy, the bridegroom came, and those who were ready went in with him to the marriage feast, and the door was shut. (Matthew 25:1–10)

It is possible to be a bridesmaid but miss the event. It is possible to avoid the full extent of the reward for our trials, simply because we "fell asleep."

Later in the chapter, Jesus tells another parable about how the church is meant to serve him. The master of the house gives each of his servants money, hoping they will invest it. Some of the servants get less than others, but the master expects the same out of them all: to do the work to invest in what he has given them.

> For it will be like a man going on a journey, who called his servants and entrusted to them his property. To one he gave five talents, to another two, to another one, to each according to his ability. Then he went away. He who had received the five talents went at once and traded with them, and he made five talents more. So also he who had the two talents made two talents more. But he who had received the one talent went and dug in the ground and hid his master's money.
>
> Now after a long time the master of those servants came and settled accounts with them. And he who had received the five talents came forward, bringing five talents more, saying, "Master, you

> delivered to me five talents; here, I have made five talents more." His master said to him, "Well done, good and faithful servant. You have been faithful over a little; I will set you over much. Enter into the joy of your master."
>
> He also who had received the one talent came forward, saying, "Master, I knew you to be a hard man, reaping where you did not sow, and gathering where you scattered no seed, so I was afraid, and I went and hid your talent in the ground. Here, you have what is yours." But his master answered him, "You wicked and slothful servant!" (Matthew 25:14–30)

God has given all of his children responsibilities while we await his return. He has given these responsibilities *to each according to their ability*. As I said earlier, God does not give us more than we can carry. Each servant was given a portion, and each was expected to invest what they could.

But the servant with the single talent did not invest at all. He called his master "hard" and said he was afraid, and so instead of investing, he buried his portion of the master's property. Sure, he had kept the money safe, but he also had gained nothing from all the time he could have been investing.

We are given chances to invest in the kingdom of heaven and to press into difficulties and opportunities as they arise. Not only this, but even our suffering is something to invest in! And what do we get for investing? Reward. But laziness and *slothfulness*, as the passage says, can steal our rewards from us. In our Christian walk, we can bury ourselves like the talent, surviving but coming out at the end with little to show. But *everything* we invest in Christ *will* reap a reward.

As I ponder these passages above, I feel the threat of a heavy burden I cannot bear. I do not quote these passages with the hope of making anyone feel guilty. The last thing any of us need is more burdens heaped on our backs. No—my exhortation is simply this: We are called to stay awake, be prepared, and invest in this life. And if we do those things, the rewards are plentiful and our characters are refined.

It seems pretty simple, right? Just stay awake, and there will be a reward. It is all well and good in theory, but in practice, I find that I am very, very, *very* human—and therefore prone to falling asleep.

Staying Awake vs. Falling Asleep

Yep, I was the girl who couldn't eat solid food. I was the girl with chronic pain. What did it mean for me to stay awake? Finally, I was attempting to face the pain and the sobering reality of my condition. I was agreeing to face my cross. But how to do this? How to face my condition with chronic pain and constant fasting with my eyes wide open?

The answer is pretty simple: In faith, I stumble forward.

As time passes, I'm realizing that there will be times where I feel full of faith and so motivated to stay awake with strength and courage. There also will be times where I just don't have it in me to care or to try. I sit around, eating foods I know will get stuck, finding excuses to not go for walks, which improve my digestion, and avoiding anyone who might interfere with my protective bubble. There's no easy answer, no flick of a wand, to make me go from sleeping to awake. It is not a matter of willpower, and it is not a matter of just giving myself a "stop being lazy" pep talk.

I am a weak, broken, but still faintly willing child of God. I need his help. And though I don't know all the reasons why, sometimes he fills me full of faith and gives me a drive to go hard into my juicing diet or go outside and walk for miles. Other times, he sits beside me while I slump with fatigue and disinterest. I say prayers like "God help me," and I don't even know what I mean.

But here is what I can do: At any given time, whether I feel strong or weak, I can ask the Lord, *Grant me strength and courage to love and serve you*. I can *ask*. And sometimes I don't have the strength to *serve*, but in those times, he just asks me to *love*.

My whole life I have been a fighter. I love a challenge and proving I can overcome it. That has made this aspect of my journey so humbling and difficult. I have had to see myself stumble over and over as I try to escape the reality of my condition. A friend—one of my Epic Ladies, who you'll meet in the next chapter—said to me today, "You have a lot of strengths, but right now God wants to minister to your weak side." I don't want a weak side, but I have one. I have one, and it is much more substantial than I want to admit. Thus, I want to feel thankful for God loving me enough to show me my weakness and how I cannot do this without him.

This is what it means to stay awake. It is to be honest about my human condition, my weaknesses, my shortcomings, and even the fatigue and depression that come from living life in a body that is breaking down. Sometimes I like to think of myself as one of the ten virgins who did bring extra oil, but she asked someone else to carry it for her: I am holding on to faith, but I can barely manage that. "The spirit is willing, but the flesh is weak" (Matthew 26:41).

All God needs is a willing heart. He can work with a willing heart. He knows how hard it is to fight the good fight when our sin nature is pulling hard against us. He knows how discouraging it is to go through constant pain.

But despite how weak we are, he *does* aid us, and he *does* help us stay awake. It is when we no longer ask him for help, or when we don't want to think about our weakness, that we fall asleep. It is when we say, "You know what? I'm done with all this suffering.

It's time to treat myself," that we choose to let the spirit inside us go to sleep, and we exist without existing, burying our talents in the dirt and choosing not to be refined by our suffering.

Yes, our suffering refines us. It's a part of Christian theology that tends to be avoided in many circles—and I get it: It feels so contradictory to say that God ordains times of suffering. It doesn't always sit well that our loving God also appoints suffering for us. But when we choose to follow Jesus, we choose the road he walked: the road of the cross, the way of suffering.

> Since therefore Christ suffered in the flesh, arm yourselves with the same way of thinking, for whoever has suffered in the flesh has ceased from sin. (1 Peter 4:1)

Our hardships sharpen us. This theme runs all through the Bible, and it doesn't have to be scary. Everyone in this world will suffer, but it is the Christian who can smile and persevere because we know there is *purpose* in our suffering. It can change and transform us—*especially* when we let it.

Trauma vs. Transformation

During this time I listened to a podcast with Jamie Winship, author of the book *Living Fearless*, where he said, "Transition involves pain."[1] It is a natural thing to experience pain with change. When change, growth, or transition comes our way, so does pain, and there are two ways of interacting with said pain: We can resist it, or we can press through it. I've summed this up as "trauma vs. transformation." Pain resisted traumatizes, and pain accepted transforms.

I did some therapy around this time, and my therapist had me do an exercise where she placed her hand against mine. When we both pushed, it was difficult and tense, and when I relaxed, I simply moved with the motion. This activity illustrates what happens when we resist pain: It hurts more. But what if this pain wasn't totally a bad thing? What if pain was evidence of a *transition*, and through it, we had a worthwhile reward?

Jamie Winship went on to say:

> Transition . . . typically causes its own suffering, or is brought about by suffering. Either way—pain, struggle, failure—is an invitation, and we . . . can look at it with a sense of joy. Like, "Okay, this is going to be hard, this is going to be awful," maybe, however, it can lead to something greater if it's . . . the way it is supposed to be. We can look at the passage about Christ looking at the heart of the cross. For the joy set before him, he endured the cross, knowing there's something beyond the pain. There is always something beyond the struggle . . . it's painful, it's discipline . . . there is something greater beyond it that's worth it.[2]

It can be so scary when we see the pain coming. For me, it often starts when I wake up in the morning, take a sip of juice, then feel an instant pain in my stomach where the G-tube once was. It's old nerve damage pain, and when it starts, I know that more pain and vomiting is probably on its way. I feel a sense of dread. Instantly, my mind searches for happy places to go and ways to avoid the trauma.

But what if this pain meant some sort of *transition?* What if it was the road to transformation? What if by pushing through the pain, I could gain a new sort of strength—a new sort of reward—simply by choosing to move forward rather than standing still?

My prayer in that moment of stomach pain is, *Lord, grant me strength and courage*. Just as Jesus needed strength and courage to face the cross, I need it every day—to face the overwhelming and terrifying prospect of future pain.

Once I throw myself on God's mercy, and in faith tell him that I want to move forward, that is when the transformation happens. As I said, all he needs is a willing heart. All he needs is for me to be willing—to be awake. And if that is true, then there is more good for me than there is evil ahead. Just like the servant who invested his talents, he will double his reward in the end and be trusted with even greater things.

I think of the strange story of when Jacob wrestled with God. A man appeared in the night and fought with Jacob:

> Jacob was left alone. And a man wrestled with him until the breaking of the day. When the man saw that he did not prevail against Jacob, he touched his hip socket, and Jacob's hip was put out of joint as he wrestled with him. Then he said, "Let me go, for the day has broken." But Jacob said, "I will not let you go unless you bless me." (Genesis 32:24–26)

When it is time to go through pain and trial, I want to be inspired by Jacob. He kept fighting until dawn, somehow knowing that this man was the Lord. He fought and would not give up.

Finally, daybreak was coming, and Jacob still held on. God had to say, "Let me go!" And Jacob's response was one of faith: "I will not go until you bless me." This is the attitude I want as I endure a trial riddled with pain: I want to hold on tight to God, saying I will not let go until I get the blessing that he has for me.

Jacob could have slept that night. Instead, he stayed awake—in fact, he didn't just stay awake, he fought. He fought so hard, God had to ask him to let go. And he held on so hard because he *knew* there was a blessing for him if he didn't let go. He wanted the reward for his perseverance, and boy, did he get it! This is when Jacob was given the name Israel and the promise that came with it. It was a rebirth for him, with a whole new identity.

This is what I mean when I say I want to stay awake. I want to be an active fighter in my trial, not someone who is being dragged along. I want to actively choose to follow Jesus down the road he has chosen, and if there is suffering, I want to hold fast to the truth that there is a blessing in it for me if I persevere.

I want to be willing, and I want to fight. Day to day, it will look different. I will have high days and low days. But I want to continually return to a willing heart—one where I can find joy when I see pain coming, knowing there is more good for me in it than there is bad.

On the night he was betrayed, Jesus asked the disciples to stay awake with him as he prayed. He was going to face the horror and agony of the cross, and despite the fact that his disciples were physically nearby, he was alone, for they fell asleep.

When I chose to follow Christ, I chose to walk the path that he walked. When I follow him, I become a fellow heir of everlasting life with him—"heirs of God and fellow heirs with Christ, *provided* we suffer with him in order that we may also be glorified with him" (Romans 8:17). When I choose to stay awake through my trials, I earn the privilege of being a disciple who did not fall asleep, doing my best to stay awake in the garden of Gethsemane, present with Jesus. When I remain sober and watchful, I experience the presence of my Lord—"Jesus, the founder and perfecter of our faith, who for the joy that was set before him endured the cross" (Hebrews 12:2).

With Jesus, I find myself crying out, "Please take this cup from me." But with Jesus, I must also cry out, "Not my will, but your will be done." With Jesus, I can face this pain with strength and courage that can only be found in relationship with him. And with Jesus, I hope to one day say, "It is finished."

The Discipline of the Lord

Living in this broken world means we will experience suffering in one way or another. Sometimes the suffering is due to other people in our life; sometimes it is a result of our own foolishness or sin; sometimes it is due to the spiritual forces that come against us, hoping to destroy us; and sometimes it is simply due to this fallen world we inherited from our father Adam.

Whether we are Christians or not, we will experience suffering. The difference between followers of Christ and other people is that followers of Christ not only have a purpose to our suffering, but I honestly believe we ultimately suffer less. I'll unpack this more later in this chapter, but for now, in short, this is because suffering without purpose is simply just that: suffering. But when suffering has a purpose, God calls it discipline. An important distinction here is that punishment is suffering due to something we have done wrong, but discipline is for our growth and maturity. This discipline is God's means of refining us, growing our character, and freeing us from our sin.

Hebrews 12 describes this discipline in a helpful and practical way, comparing the Lord's discipline with that of a parent:

> "My son, do not regard lightly the discipline of the Lord, nor be weary when reproved by him. For the Lord disciplines the one he loves, and chastises every son whom he receives."
>
> It is for discipline that you have to endure. God is treating you as sons. For what son is there whom his father does not discipline? If you are left without discipline, in which all have participated, then you are illegitimate children and not sons. (Hebrews 12:5–6)

This passage very clearly explains that being a child of God means being disciplined by him. Outside of his oversight, we would be left to wallow in our sins and foolishness. We would be left to figure out what it means to thrive on our own. We would still suffer, but that suffering would result in more brokenness, rather than less. But when God is our Father, we can know that anything unpleasant he allows is intentional, and it is evidence of his care for us.

This reminds me of parenting my youngest child. There are times when I have less of myself to give, especially when I am experiencing intense health struggles. And in those times, I check her less, I discipline her less, and as a result, she gets herself into more trouble. For her, it might feel great, because she isn't facing correction or consequences for her behavior. In times like those, what she needs is more of me. In times like those, my love for her compels me to press in and be more involved in her day-to-day life.

I do not give this same care to children that are not my own. I may witness certain behaviors in other children that could benefit from some dedicated attention, but it would not be my place to do it. But what a comfort it is that God says to me, "I am your Father," and, "I discipline the ones I love, and chastise every child whom I receive." It is no accident that I am experiencing hardship, despite the fact that I am a Christian. As it says above, my chastisement is evidence of who my good Father is.

Verses 9–10 explain just how hopeful and effective this discipline is.

> Besides this, we have had earthly fathers who disciplined us and we respected them. Shall we not much more be subject to the Father of spirits and live? For they disciplined us for a short time as it seemed best to them, but he disciplines us for our good, that we may share his holiness. For the moment all discipline seems painful rather than pleasant, but later it yields the peaceful fruit of righteousness to those who have been trained by it. (Hebrews 12:9–10)

This passage makes me think back on my own parenting again. I find it reassuring that God knows I do the best I can, and yet what I do is not perfect. Sometimes my kids will benefit from my leadership, and sometimes I will let them down. They might be hurt by me. They might suffer because of my mistakes. This is what it means to be an earthly parent, and it's hard to come to terms with that. But God contrasts his discipline with ours in this way: What we do is sometimes good, and sometimes harmful; what God does is *always* good, and to those who have been trained by it, it *always* yields fruit in us.

What a relieving thought this is! I am smiling to myself as I write this. God's discipline is good! As his child, I can know that he will discipline me perfectly. He will not do *anything* that will not benefit me. This means that I do not have to be afraid when he doesn't always take away the scary or painful things that come my way. I can trust that he will train me perfectly.

And why is this discipline so good? Why is it worth it in the end? *"That we may share his holiness."* He is making us like himself, and *that* is what it means to truly thrive.

All of God's discipline is good. So let us, as Hebrews says, "be trained by it"! Let us not resist his good parenting, but listen and treasure his oversight. His discipline yields the "peaceful fruit of righteousness."

It's pretty amazing to think that the way to peace is often through the path of suffering. It might sound a little backwards. When I try to avoid suffering, I am doing it because I want to maintain my peace. But it is *through* my trials that I will find true peace, and that is an encouraging thought.

Hebrews 12 brings this whole passage to a beautiful exhortation. They are the sort of verses that compel me into motion, making me want to fight for the prize that is on the other side of my trial:

> Therefore lift your drooping hands and strengthen your weak knees, and make straight paths for your feet, so that what is lame may not be put out of joint but rather be healed. (Hebrews 12:12–13)

One of the scariest things about suffering is the idea that I am going to be hurt. And if life were really only about the physical, then this would be a very concerning truth. But God is not just concerned with our physical state; he is also concerned with our spiritual state. His discipline exists to heal me, not to hurt me. And this passage implores me to not give up because of this! I've reworded this passage with a message for myself as I try hard to grasp on to the truth of it:

Don't hang your arms in hopelessness, Tasha. Keep moving forward without fear of this path taking you down an impossible road. I am not going to worsen your pain and turn it into a debilitating wound; I am going to *heal* you.

The path that we think is there to harm us is the path of healing. And I can know that this is true because God is my Father.

I can't help but think of Jacob when I hear the phrase, "put out of joint." When this man wrestled with God all through the night, it could have seemed like God was against Jacob. This couldn't be further from the truth. His leg was truly wounded, and his character was softened and refined after that day. For a long time I have held on to the story of Jacob. For a good part of my adulthood, I have walked with a cane because my connective tissue disease also destroyed my left hip joint. But his story and this passage in Hebrews is a reminder to me that my hip injury wasn't just meaningless pain; God used it and still uses it as a reminder that he is my Father. Physically, I may not be fixed. But this road I am on is one of healing, and every little thing God allows me to go through will do me good if I allow myself to be trained by it.

God's Oversight vs. No Oversight

Building on the idea that God disciplines us for our good, I truly believe that submitting ourselves to God as his children ultimately means we will suffer less. Yes, we will suffer, but (1) not without it doing us ultimate good, and (2) not beyond what we can bear. First Corinthians 10:13 states:

> God is faithful, and he will not let you be tempted beyond your ability, but with the temptation he will also provide the way of escape, that you may be able to endure it. (1 Corinthians 10:13)

Temptation, trial, suffering, hardship—God does not take his children through anything he will not also give them the strength and the faith to bear. Just as I, as a parent, will not give my child a task or a chore that I don't think they can accomplish, while also giving them whatever aid they might need, God will guide and protect his children in a loving and perfect way.

Our Father is not just one who disciplines us; he also protects and rescues us from danger. Psalm 34 beautifully states:

> When the righteous cry for help, the Lord hears
> and delivers them out of all their troubles.
> The Lord is near to the brokenhearted
> and saves the crushed in spirit.
> Many are the afflictions of the righteous,
> but the Lord delivers him out of them all. (Psalm
> 34:17–19)

If it is true that our Father will not allow us to go through any suffering that will not do ultimate good in us, that means he will deliver us from anything and everything that will do us harm. He rescues us from evil, and even when our own foolishness leads us into danger, he will deliver us!

This really sets us as God's children apart from the rest of the world. While others may be thrown about by the waves of evil in this world, we are preserved and protected. This makes me want to run into the arms of my Savior all the more. Why would I avoid his leading and oversight when he is the only one who can spare me from true evil?

In 2 Samuel, King David directly disobeys the Lord's command and takes a census of the people of Israel. God is angry and sends a messenger to David, telling him he must choose his punishment. God gives David three choices: pestilence, famine, and being chased by Israel's enemies. Dismayed, David says, "I am in great distress. Let us fall into the hand of the LORD, for his mercy is great; but let me not fall into the hand of man" (2 Samuel 24:14).

David was facing true consequences for his disobedience. And even then, he chose pestilence, knowing that this was a force that God would control. He contrasts suffering from the Lord with suffering inflicted by other people, saying that the Lord's mercy is great.

With God, there is mercy. No matter what the cause of my suffering may be, I want God to be the one who oversees it.

We will suffer. This is a fact. In this world, we will suffer. Without God, we are subject to the evil that is in man, the evil that is in our own sin, and the evil of our spiritual enemy. So let us suffer under the oversight of God, knowing that he is merciful and loving.

This may require us to come to terms with the fact that God is working through our pain. But for me—for someone who must face pain every single day—it is a comfort. It is a relief, knowing that when I am with the Lord, and even when I am facing this debilitating and painful condition, I am ultimately suffering *less* than I would otherwise.

Keeping this kind of mindset is one way of staying awake. It is a way of confessing and acknowledging the truth that God is at work in my life and I can be trained by it. Even when I don't have the strength or drive to seize the day, God is still at work in me. He does the work, not me. All I have to do is choose to participate in it, even if all it means is saying, "Not my will, but your will be done."

Choosing the Fast

Grant us strength and courage to love and serve you.

Choosing to truly fast, to feel the pain and to walk in the way of the cross, is what it means for me, for now, to love and serve my Lord. When others tell me "you should not be in pain," I wish they would say instead: "If Jesus does not deliver you from the pain, then he is allowing it for your good. He will give you the strength and courage to love and serve him in the midst of it, and the reward *will* be worth it."

The pain doesn't seem so terrible if it can accomplish something good in me. The shears don't seem so horrifying once that dying branch has been clipped away. This pain may or may not traumatize me, but it can also *transform* me.

Strength and courage. That is what I must ask for. Lord, give me the strength and the courage to walk with you on this path. When I chose Jesus, and to walk in his footsteps—to walk in the way that leads to eternal life—I chose the way of the cross. I chose a road with suffering.

> Then Jesus told his disciples, "If anyone would come after me, let him deny himself and take up his cross and follow me. For whoever would save his life will lose it, but whoever loses his life for my sake will find it." (Matthew 16:24–25)

This road we walk is one we walk with Jesus. And when we stay awake and active in our suffering, we are staying awake with him. And not only is this a comfort to us, but it is a comfort to him, too.

My mother is a fervent and devoted follower of Jesus, and she has been an example to me of what it looks like to faithfully walk the road of the cross. For as long as I could remember, she never drank alcohol. When I was a child, it didn't seem to be all that big of a fast. There was never liquor in our home. But as I reached adulthood, alcohol became more common in my home. Wine would be served at family events, and my siblings and I would enjoy cocktails on rainy nights. Still, there my mother would be, sitting seemingly on the outside, drinking apple cider.

It's a fast she has never broken. And as someone who has been drinking for most of my adult life, I am more aware of how difficult that actually is. As an adult, when I have asked her why she fasts, this is the essence of what she tells me: "Jesus is fasting from wine, and I want to fast with him. It is an opportunity for me to suffer and wait with him. When he asked his disciples to stay awake with him, he was alone. In this way, I am able to be with him."

Facing the pain is a form of fasting. Choosing not to fight against the trial is a form of fasting. It is denying ourselves what we wish was happening, or what we wish wasn't happening, and choosing to be content with the suffering before us. It is a form of faith when we trust God that he will work in the hardest things, and his work will always yield fruit.

I want to keep choosing the fast. I want to keep submitting myself to the road God chooses for me, knowing he loves me and that this road is better than all other roads. On this road, I will ultimately suffer the least; on this road, I will be refined; on this road, I will find joy; and on this road is where Jesus walks.

— 6 —

finding contentment

With gladness and singleness of heart

I began writing this chapter on a day when I felt the least amount of gladness or singleness of heart that I have ever felt. I continually broke down in tears, saying things like, "I don't want this," "This isn't fair," "I hate this," and "Why is my life so full of *no's*?"

I was sitting on my bed, thinking of anything I could possibly do to make myself feel happier. It was the day after Thanksgiving, and I wasn't able to eat the feast, which was excruciating. It was also my first Thanksgiving after choosing to give up drinking alcohol for a time; that was difficult, as I associated it with so many happy memories. And it was the week that my hands started to tremble so much that I wasn't able to write or draw almost anything. Even in these two paragraphs, I made a kazillion typos and attempts at fixing them. We had discovered that a part of my condition involves small fiber neuropathy—the gradual death of my peripheral nervous system. As I laid on my bed crying, Lindsay came in to talk to me. I told him, "I just feel so empty."

I texted my "Epic Ladies," three women who have committed to going through life together, chasing Jesus and learning how to thrive in him. I texted them asking them to pray for me as I tried to face the fact that my condition may take away my ability to write and draw at some point in my life—perhaps much sooner than I thought. I told them that this all comes right before Christmas, when we are struggling to pay all of the medical bills. I told them, I *just* can't smile anymore. I am so sad.

Amid the confusion, disillusion, grief, and overall sadness that my friends expressed in response, one of them said this:

> This storm threatens to upset a deep sense of peace. And God is inviting you, saying, "What if you trust me to provide for you in this now? What if your best life is following me down this road?" There are certain kinds of provision, protection, and empowerment that only happen when we surrender. We don't know where God is going to take us, but we know in whom we trust. We trust in his character and his power. So we invest in him, not the world, for our help. What if Jesus is inviting you to trust him in a deeper way?

She said these things with the caveat that she herself is struggling to trust God with what is happening to me in this trial. She and many others who love me have watched me lose feasts and health, one by one. I lost the feasting of food; I lost the ability to go to many public events—and now, I am facing the possibility of losing one of my most cherished joys: the ability to communicate.

This neurological component—involving numbness, migraines, dysmotility in other digestive organs, shaking of hands, and even slurring of speech—adds a new wave of loss and many more questions as to what else I might lose as it develops. I do not know if it is temporary or progressive, but on a day like today, I struggle to face it. I choose to write today, despite my grief, to give you a snapshot of where my heart goes on days like this, when I must deal with the reality of this disease.

Amid my recent difficulties, I have tried to cling to the ability to write, draw, and tell stories. But this last week, my hands were too shaky to draw; my mouth continued to slur and chomp when I tried to speak; and I kept dropping my pencil. *Why, God?* I ask. *Why would you ever take away such a thing?* I have become like Job, sitting in silence amid the storm of loss, scratching my boils with clay. What have I become? God, where are you in *all* of this?

Jesus doesn't promise we will be glad and have singleness of heart when trials like this come our way. In fact, in faith, I have chosen to write this chapter today of all days, when it feels the most impossible to be glad and have a steady heart giving me singleness of mind.

But that's the thing: Gladness and *singleness of heart* aren't things that I myself can muster. They are not something I am able to conjure up when I need them. This is not a pull-up-your-bootstraps kind of command. *Gladness* and *singleness of heart* are only found in Jesus. *He* holds them, and the only way for me to grasp them is to grasp the hem of his cloak.

I imagine my life lately as if I am on a road. Jesus has led me through some dark forests, but he has also protected me and equipped me to keep walking. But right now, it is as if I have come to a dead stop as he points his lantern toward the valley of the shadow of death and says, "Now, we go this way."

I resist. I shrink away from this new path. There is evil down that road. It is evil that threatens to take away the things that give me the *most* gladness. It threatens to take away the things that help anchor me and give me *singleness of heart*. It threatens to debilitate my hands, keeping me from writing; it threatens to take away my lips and inhibit my brain, keeping me from communicating with the ones I love. Why would he *ever* lead me down this road?

But there he goes, walking carefully into the valley, looking back at me as if to ask: Do you trust me?

I don't think I have ever replied "no" to those words, and I have heard him ask me this question many times in my life. But this time, it feels different. I feel him asking me to trust him when *all* things might be taken away. I see him pointing down the road that leads to the cross, and I see him telling me to pick up that cross. He isn't just asking me to give him my life; he is asking me to give him my very being. He wants me to trust him that gladness follows him and that if I follow him, I too will be content and somehow have *singleness of heart.*

Singleness of Heart

I am flipping the words in the prayer so that I can address singleness of heart first and gladness after. I believe that it is the singleness of heart that begets—or rather, *opens the door*—to gladness.

Have you ever found yourself saying, "I have two minds about it" when trying to make a decision or "I'm feeling divided" in a conversation about one of your convictions? Lindsay and I are a couple who like to process new ideas together. We bring up a thought, then try asking questions and looking at it from all angles. We say things like, "One side of me is compelled by this idea, but another side of me feels really cautious and concerned." We discuss our feelings, asking what is valid and what is flawed. We work together until we find ourselves on the same page.

Being on the same page as a couple makes us feel unified. It means that, when conflicts and questions are brought our way, we feel that we are *of the same mind.* That's been a theme in our marriage. We are so focused on being *of the same mind* that we will talk for hours, if that's what it takes, in order to get on the same page. It's made for a very peaceful marriage. It's made for the sort of marriage that makes us feel as though the other person really *is* a part of the same body and the same *mind.*

Because Lindsay and I do our best to practice *singleness of heart* in our marriage, I want to use our marriage as an example in this chapter. But I want to make something very clear: All marriages are different, each with different challenges and strengths. I am not writing this in order to be compared with others but simply to tell my story, using parts of my life as an example.

Singleness of heart. I want to take a moment to give you a picture of what *singleness of heart* is like for Lindsay and me. Lindsay and I developed a good system for how to help me reform my relationship with alcohol. For a time, he held the key to the liquor cabinet, and on special occasions, when we thought I could be free to indulge, only he would pour the drink, and I would never touch the bottle. This wasn't because I was detoxing from true alcoholism. Thank the Lord, it never went in that direction, though I admit it could have. No, we simply wanted the world to feel safe for me as I struggled through letting go of my liquid feast. It was hard for me. Without eating solids, alcohol felt so special. So rather than forcing me to be strong and say no whenever I opened the liquor cabinet, Lindsay took on the task of standing as a protective barrier between me and the substance that I was giving up for a time.

The other day, we were sitting and painting together, and I looked up at Lindsay and said, "I am really missing when I used to have my Saturday cocktail. What do you think about me having one just this week?"

I knew what his answer would be, but I asked anyway. I was, so to speak, leaning on the proverbial fence that was keeping me from falling into a ravine.

Lindsay looked at me with a smile. "Well," he said, "I think you know what I am going to say, Tasha."

"Say it anyway," I said. "I need to hear it."

"I think it would be a bad idea. You decided to say no to this, and you asked me to say no, too. So that's what I am going to say: no."

I smiled. Relief washed over my sadness and the anger that still fought against this no. We both felt the tension of my tricky circumstance, but it was the singleness of mind that set us free from the battle. We had both decided to walk a certain road, and when a tempting path opened up, compelling me to leave that road, Lindsay was able to say, "Remember what we decided?"

It was easier for me to say no to a change in course when we had already agreed on a route. This is something I call "contentment through limitations." The fences and barriers that we put up on our road kept us single-hearted as we walked a tricky path. It wasn't an easy path to walk, but it was the path we chose. It is so much easier to be content in life when we have chosen our particular circumstances. We chose limitations; we chose our battle. We agreed to give up alcohol together for a time, and it gave us single-heartedness to fight through the battle with our eyes on the prize.

I suppose I am switching metaphors, moving from a path chosen to a battle chosen. But that is what it's like. If you imagine choosing a hard path with constant goblin attacks (yes, somehow every metaphor turns into fantasy in my mind), then you are going to anticipate their attacks and feel the drive to fight them when they come. If you had not knowingly chosen this battle-wrought path, you might have chosen to flee to another road when danger showed its ugly face. But no, you chose the path that you knew led to a great treasure. You want that treasure, so you brave the danger.

A path chosen is easier to walk than a path wandered into. Singleness of heart is the happy result of a choice made; a clear direction chosen that makes other hurdles and encounters bearable. We have singleness of heart when we know where we are going and why we are going there.

Now we get to the heart of it. Imagine I am walking a path with a guide. I am being led down a goblin-infested path. I have been on many roads with this particular guide. He has kept me safe from the most dangerous and life-threatening situations, but he has also led me down the paths with the rarest of riches and the most glorious yields. He is the guide of all guides. I have been on enough adventures with him that I trust him with my very life.

But now this guide is suggesting the most dangerous path of all. There are no longer just goblins but trolls and demons. There are terrors that have destroyed many brave and legendary adventurers. All the other guides say that this path will kill me, that there is no hope, that I will lose all the riches I gained on every other journey. They try to detour me.

But this legendary guide is Jesus. And he is calling me down a path that doesn't just take away food but could take away my hands, my lips, even my *mind*.

"Trust me," he says, "you will be safe; I will be with you. There are even greater riches if you let me hold your hand."

It will take *singleness of heart* to follow him. *Singleness of heart* means choosing him as a guide. It means walking where he walks; stopping where he stops; crying when he is crying; and rejoicing when he rejoices.

One of my Epic Ladies recently hiked Mount Kilimanjaro. When she took the time to describe the experience to the rest of us, I was floored by the amount of effort and trust it took. She braved times of vomiting and crippling headaches from elevation sickness and other times where she could hardly breathe. Their guide told her when to rest and told her when to move. The peak of the mountain had so little air that they were only allowed to see the view for a certain amount of time. She could die if she didn't listen to her guide. When he said, "Time to leave," they left. There were times when others on her trek wanted to stop, but the guide said no.

Singleness of mind does not require us to want to follow the orders of our perfect guide, Jesus. It simply requires that we *do* follow, that we obey. We may not like where he leads, but a single heart chooses to go because it trusts its guide. We trust in Jesus, and that is what makes it possible to obey, even if our every emotion and sensation screams at us to run the other way.

There is no great secret to *singleness of mind*. It is simply a choice. Jesus *is* leading me down a road I don't want to go. And I can fight him, kicking and screaming the whole way, or I can try running down alternate paths which promise ease and comfort or, at the very least, numbness. But if I actually trust that Jesus is the source of goodness and *gladness*, then I will choose him. I will choose the suffering and the loss that he leads me through, trusting that he will give me everything I need in order to thrive in this trial.

Gladness

So, let's say you have chosen the right guide. You have chosen to cling to his side, following his lead, knowing that when you are with him, you will be able to thrive. You have singleness of heart.

You may have noticed, I am hesitant to promise things like "you will be *okay,*" because the idea of being okay is vague and implies certain feelings and expectations. I use the word *thrive* instead, because I think this is what Jesus promises us. Like a healthy childbirth with straightforward circumstances, a woman can be in *pain* but also be *thriving* at the same time.

So you have chosen to thrive, to walk the path of suffering that Jesus walks. You have access to the treasures and resources he has in his keep. He holds in his hands the thing which you crave most in hard times: He holds gladness.

We live in a world that is addicted and enslaved to the pursuit of gladness, despite the fact that it very seldom delivers on its promise. Whether Costco promises gladness for your child if you buy them the big playhouse; or McDonald's promises gladness when you get to bite into that burger you've been craving all day; or the new season of *The Great British Baking Show* promises gladness when you watch other people live out your dream; or your diligence promises you gladness after working hard to sleep-train your baby; or money promises gladness when you finally get to buy the thing you've always wanted—do any of these things last? Do they give you anything but a moment of gladness, leaving you feeling empty sometime after? Do any of these pursuits make good on their promises?

No, what our culture gives us instead are a million ways to try to *solve* our lack of gladness. Like a beggar standing on the roadside, collecting pennies from passersby, they may collect enough to buy a sandwich and satiate their immediate hunger, but they still begin the next day on that same roadside, holding out their empty bowl and cradling their empty stomach.

Still, we believe that these momentary installments will bring us joy and contentment. We visit restaurants, doctors, friends, parties, gyms, and we praise these places for giving us a reason to get out of bed in the morning. We are addicted to the pursuit of gladness, but we very seldom experience the real thing.

True gladness is found in a person. It is found when we choose to actually be present with that person, sitting where he sits, walking where he walks, avoiding what he avoids, and looking at him right in the eyes when we feel ourselves wanting to leave his side. Gladness comes from the contentment that only Jesus offers. When you choose to take up your cross and follow him, you make a choice: You choose a path, and that means choosing *everything* that is on that path. There may be pain; there may be trials; there may be climbs that you thought you could never complete; but there is also gladness. There is hope, there is peace, there is contentment, and there is *life*.

I think of *gladness* as **joy found in the present provisions and person of Jesus.** Gladness rejoices in reality—in what is truly given to us—like a child who waited twenty-five days (or perhaps 364 days) for Christmas and then finally got to open their presents. As they peel back the paper and look at what has been given freely to them, they are glad.

I truly believe that, in every moment of our life with Christ, there is a present to be enjoyed. There is something good and pure being offered to us at this very moment. It may not be what we wanted or expected, but it is there. If we receive it as exactly what it is, we may experience true gladness.

It might not feel how we expect gladness to feel. For example, when a friend urged me to start exercising, she told me how great I would feel when I did it. If I am honest, I hated it for the first eight weeks that I started going for daily jogs. But after my body and mind settled into the new routine, I began to find the gladness that this practice offered me. As I ran, moved my body, and sweated, I let the gift be what it was rather than what I expected it to be. And at that point, I could find true gladness in it. Yes, true gladness rejoices in what is actually given, rather than what we wanted or expected.

In C. S. Lewis' book *Perelandra*, Ransom, the protagonist, stumbles across a tree in the new world he is exploring. He eats its fruit and is overcome with euphoria at the experience of its taste. A short time later, he finds another tree and, expecting the same experience as the following time, he finds himself disappointed, despite the fact that this second fruit is also delicious. His expectations had tempted him to reject a good thing. This soberingly illustrates our refusal to receive gifts from God: We reject the fruit that is given because we didn't get the fruit we expected.

We are given good things when we walk with Jesus. He has gladness and contentment in his keep. Day by day, these gifts are offered to us, though we often dismiss them, turning up our noses at their lack of expected luster.

We are like children, leaving the safety of our backyard because we are convinced there is more fun elsewhere. What if we stopped chasing gladness and played on the ordinary playset in our backyard? What if we just sat in the place that is already ours—already given—and saw the beauty therein: The blackbirds hopping in the grass, the clouds changing shape, and the joy that comes from enjoying what is already ours?

As parents, we commend our children when we see them choosing to enjoy the dinner prepared for them rather than wishing they could have had a burger from McDonald's. We smile and say, "This is good! They are learning contentment!" And then, we go upstairs and say, "I wish I had McDonald's," feeling our own discontentment seeping in.

Jesus is the parent compelling us to forget the burger and enjoy the meal he made for us. He is sitting down in the middle of the valley of the shadow of death, spreading out a picnic blanket.

"Sit with me," he says, patting the ground. He sets up a lantern, which provides an orb of safe light for us to sit beside him. He lays out a dinner of bread and pours us a cup of wine. It overflows. "Sit with me," he says. "What I have is good."

At this point, you could choose to wander, looking for better offers, or you could sit. And there in the valley, sitting with your competent and trustworthy Guide, there is an opportunity for true joy. If you are willing to sit and receive what is actually offered, you will receive the gift of gladness.

As I said above, I have chosen to write this chapter on the worst of all days. Today I am the traveler who is dying for the cushioned seats of a McDonald's and angry about the wounds that feel as though they will kill me. I don't want to be in the present; I want to run away. I want to be anywhere but here!

But still, I chose to sit down. And here, in this moment of quiet contemplation, I am writing these words, with the faith that they are true: that there is indeed gladness for me in the person of Christ.

I am crying as I write this. I have him. Forget what is in the package he held out for me—*he* is here! The person who is the source of all gladness, the source of all riches, and the creator of everything I think I need. *He* is with me. He is better than the reward at the end of this road; he is the reward. I get him *now*. I call to mind the passage that my heart and mind continually return to in my struggle against pain and emptiness. From Lamentations 3:13–24:

> He drove into my kidneys
> the arrows of his quiver;
> I have become the laughingstock of all my people,
> the object of their taunts all day long.
> He has filled me with bitterness;
> he has sated me with wormwood.
> He has made my teeth grind on gravel,
> and made me cower in ashes;
> my soul is bereft of peace;
> I have forgotten what happiness is;
> so I say, "My endurance has perished;
> so has my hope from the Lord."
> Remember my affliction and my wanderings,
> the wormwood and the gall!
> My soul continually remembers it
> and is bowed down within me.
> But this I call to mind,
> and therefore I have hope:
> The steadfast love of the Lord never ceases;
> his mercies never come to an end;

they are new every morning;
great is your faithfulness.
"The LORD is my portion," says my soul,
"therefore I will hope in him."

The Lord is my portion. In the midst of so much pain and sadness, *he* is my portion. He is my gift; he is what makes my heart glad. This is such a profound truth, said in the simplest of ways. Why would I choose to walk the path of pain and fasting, the path of a disease that might take away the use of my hands? I will walk the path because he is on it with me, because I want *him*. He is the treasure. He is the pearl of great price. In him is all gladness; in him there is singleness of heart.

The Gift of the Present

In this chapter, I planned on leaving my reader with a gift. I wanted to give you a thirst for true contentment. I wanted to exhort you to face your life with Christ with gladness and singleness of heart. Whether he leads you through paths of abundance or paths of danger and trial, I wanted you to seek one thing: contentment. But there is something more important than contentment. There is the *source* of contentment and the One who can actually enable us to find contentment in any time or place or circumstance. There is the presence and person of Christ.

Earlier I defined gladness as joy found in the present provisions and person of Jesus. Jesus is with you in this present moment. He has gifts unique to today that may only be received today, like manna in the wilderness. Will you look away, feeling disappointed by their inability to meet your expectations? Or will you find joy in today's unique gifts, receiving them with a glad heart?

Let me leave you with this picture from Psalm 23. Imagine Jesus as your guide on the road I described, that perilous road that leads to worthwhile treasure. *The Lord is my guide; I shall not want.* In the keep of our Savior, Jesus Christ, you have everything you need. Food, safety, clothing, and life. On this journey, all your needs will be provided. *Even though I walk through the valley of the shadow of death, I will fear no evil, for you are with me.*

You sit with your guide, Jesus, on that road through the valley of the shadow of death. You have followed him on this road, because you trust him. You trust in who he is, and you trust that he has true thriving for you, held in his hands on this very day—in this very moment. In the midst of the dark valley, and with enemies who would do you harm, lurking among the shadows, he lays out a picnic blanket. *You prepare a table before me in the presence of my enemies.*

So you sit down, and he brings out the bread and the wine. *My cup overflows.* There, in the middle of the terrors which threaten to kill you, you *feast*. In the last place you could ever expect to enjoy yourself, you are given a *feast*!

You feel tempted to distract yourself from the shadows and the whispers that taunt you in the night. You consider making yourself drunk on the wine of your overflowing cup. You want to place your hands over your ears and mutter sounds to yourself so that you do not have to think about where you are.

Your guide taps you on your knee, compelling you to be present with him. Do you ignore him, closing your eyes and stopping your ears? Or do you brave the reality of your surroundings and lower your hands so that you might see and hear him? Do you gulp down the wine, dulling your senses enough to not *care* that you are in the valley? Or do you remain sober, with a mind that is able to comprehend the words your guide might say?

Jesus holds out a wrapped gift for you. It is something you may only open if you have your eyes open and your ears unstopped. This is the gift: the gift of the present. There is beauty that can only be received *in* the valley, on this *very* night, from *this* exact guide, and with a sober mind. In this gift is true beauty, true wholeness, and true contentment. Yes, you are in a dark place, and yes, your body hurts, but you are *still* given a feast.

Be single-hearted in the moment you are in. And in that place of raw, unfiltered, and unveiled reality, be glad. Be glad because here—exactly where you are—there is a feast.

A Glimpse of the Feast

Last night, I began to decorate for Christmas. It is the day of the year when it is my tradition to open a bottle of wine, blast Sia's Christmas album, and decorate like there is no tomorrow. Some of my children were making paper snowflakes with my cousin Sophia; my godsister Becca was putting together ornament crafts with the others; and Lindsay had just brought in my Christmas storage tubs. As I began to unravel the garlands, my spirit sank.

I looked around at all the excitement as the Christmas music began to play, and I felt the lack.

"I just realized," I said aloud to the room, "this is my first Christmas not drinking. I always celebrate by opening a bottle of wine. It . . . it feels really hard."

Lindsay, Becca, and Sophia looked at each other, then Lindsay said, "Why don't you make a fancy mocktail, and we will all drink it together?"

My heart didn't leap with excitement at the idea. I wanted wine. Wine always made me so happy—made the decorating even more joy-filled—or *did* it? The lie began to crack as I resigned myself to making a mocktail. I had mint growing in the garden, limes in the fridge, and fruit in the freezer. I could make a mocktail.

I drank the mocktail in my nice crystal. I told myself to try to receive *the fruit that I had been given*, rather than *the fruit I had expected*. Perhaps if I wasn't comparing this mocktail to the wine I usually had on decorating day, I might actually enjoy it!

The mocktail was fine. It wasn't fantastic, but it was fine. And as I strung up garlands and lights, I watched as my children's eyes ignited with the excitement of truly the most wonderful time of the year.

I wanted the wine because the alcohol usually embellished the feeling of happiness on a night like that one. At least, that was what I had always told myself. In reality, in the later hours of the night, I often grew cranky and tired, snapped easily, and withdrew. That's what alcohol does: It pulls us away from the present, and then as it wears off, it gives us a sense of urgency to escape the present further by shutting everything down.

The truth is, the happiness I felt every year on decorating night came from the true gifts my Lord always had for me, not from drink. Alcohol didn't *embellish* the gift that God had already said was good; it actually *stole* from it. Alcohol waters down joy like too much water to hot cocoa mix: You think you are adding to the volume of enjoyment, when in reality you are creating a tasteless, festive beverage of hot nothing.

What if every year I had missed out on part of the true gift? What if, instead of a pint of flavorless brown water, I could have had a small, espresso-sized, chocolate delicacy, something so special it is only available once a year?

By choosing to let go of the lie that alcohol made me happier, I let myself enjoy the actual gift that last night was. I had intentional conversations; I was able to be aware of my children's different emotions and reactions; I actually *felt* the thrill of my rendezvous with Lindsay under the mistletoe; and I had more than one moment just sitting, sipping hot cider, looking around at the magical scene around me.

This, I thought to myself as I sat there, *is what so many people wish they could have on Christmas. And to think that I felt the need to distance myself from it through alcohol. I might have missed this. I might have missed this, but I didn't. This is my feast. Thank you, Jesus.*

I face a life which threatens to take away everything. This disease threatens to steal my ability to write books like this one, to illustrate more FatCat books, and to communicate with my own children and husband on future Christmases. That future feels impossible and hopeless. But my hope can't be rooted in outcomes and anticipations. My hope is found in today, where Jesus is. If all I am doing is wishing for other times, places, or feasts I have built up in my mind, then my life really will look hopeless. But when I am in the moment, sitting with my Guide and looking him in the eyes, then I have hope.

He asks me to continue down this road of lack with gladness and singleness of heart. It sounds almost cruel to say those words, but it's not. It is not cruel for Jesus to offer gladness and singleness of heart. He is a good guide—a good shepherd, as Jesus calls himself. He will be with me, and that is how I am able to write this chapter. It is as if he moves my fingers to type as I pray inwardly, "I believe; Lord, help my unbelief."

Yes, we can be content in the face of deep lack. In fact, to be content *is* to lack. It is to lack, and yet say, "I have enough." When we say "yes" to the gifts Jesus has for us, it means saying "no" to everything else. It means believing that Jesus wants good for us, even when he takes things away.

In him there is no lack, for his love fills every empty space. He is my portion; he is my prize; he is my feast; and he is enough.

7

feasting

Through Christ our Lord

It was the first Easter following my first year of not being able to eat. Our parish met on the Saturday night prior in order to welcome Easter with a feast. We all brought foods that we had fasted from for the last forty days, and since our family had once again fasted from meat, we brought teriyaki chicken—a Washington-state staple. I wasn't super great at planning ahead at this point, so I went to the feast anticipating finding foods that I might be able to swallow. The selection wasn't easy to work with, and after trying a few different soft foods, I spent the end of the feast purging.

Something felt so wrong. It was Easter—the big feast for which all the fasting had prepared our hearts for. It was Easter, and I was the only one still fasting.

"Always Lent, never Easter," Lindsay said sympathetically. The two of us struggled to know how to rejoice that Easter. It felt so wrong to still be broken on the day that we sang triumphant songs about resurrected bodies!

I remember looking around at the Easter service the next morning, watching the other people in the room. We have a good mix of ages in our parish, ranging from newborn babies to ninety-year-old Father Bruce. It was the grayer heads that I noticed that morning. Some sat because they couldn't stand; some leaned on canes; some served communion; some raised their hands in praise. I saw a family with a grown daughter in a wheelchair; I saw a woman with a head covering, following her most recent chemo treatment. I was not the only broken person that Easter. I was not the only one with the constant reminder that my body had not yet been resurrected. I was not the only person fasting on a feast day. And yet, there I was, charged by Christ himself to enjoy the feast.

How? How could I feast when I could not eat?

Living a Mosaic of Fasting and Feasting

Feasting is good. I cannot say this enough. I speak so highly about fasting in this book that I feel I might be in danger of being accused of being against feasts. There is no way McTasha will ever be against feasts—I am a feaster, and I always will be. I may be going through a big lesson in learning to appreciate fasting; and I may be detoxing from unhealthy idolatry around feasting; but I *am* a feaster!

One of my Epic Ladies identifies herself as being "the one you will find in the house of mourning rather than the house of feasting." We laugh together about how hard it is for me to enter into sadness, while she finds it hard to, as she puts it, "stop and smell the roses." Perhaps this chapter is for those like her, who admit to needing a vision for what it might look like for a Christian to enjoy feasting in a world as broken as the one we live in. She finds it hard to turn a blind eye to the brokenness and wonders how we are supposed to rejoice—as Samwise the Brave put it in *The Two Towers* movie—"after so much bad has happened."[1]

The truth is, whether a Christian is drawn more strongly to fasting or to feasting, we need to taste them both in order to experience the fullness of the Christian life.

When Adam and Eve disregarded God's good intentions for them and the world by eating the forbidden fruit, sin rushed in and infected every part of creation. This is what theologians call the fall.

The fall took God's beautiful glass ornament of the world and threw it on the ground, shattering it into a hundred, irreparable pieces. Humanity's very nature and our physical bodies were now destined for pain and death. *The Theology of Illness* by Jean-Claude Larchet emphasizes how the broken state of our bodies forced humankind to see suffering as only a negative—something leading only to death: "Man and nature have become a battlefield where evil and good, death and life, wage a permanent, merciless combat against each other. This combat is made evident by sickness, infirmity and suffering; and until the Incarnation of Christ, its outcome was uncertain."[2] Before Christ came, the ornament was sadly broken, laying on the floor in pieces. But through his incarnation, Jesus brought with him hope for our physical and spiritual brokenness.

Jesus was the glue that held the pieces of that ornament together, now in the form of a mosaic. He recrafted the orb, allowing the broken pieces to form an ornament again. The world has a million cracks and a whole lot of grouting that had not been there before the fall, but the ornament is *still* beautiful.

A day will come when the shards of this glass ornament will be melted down and re-blown into a new, perfect orb. Its beauty, with new colors and contours characterized from its time as a mosaic, will surpass that of the first ornament. It will have the purity of the original but a maturity and nuance of design that could not have existed in something new and untested.

I will use this imagery as I talk about feasting in this chapter: the three ornaments—the original bauble, the mosaic bauble, and the bauble to come. The first is perfect; the second is flawed; the third is perfected. All three are beautiful, and the beauty of all three should be admired.

If fasting is walking along the colorless trails of grouting that hold the ornament together, then feasting is when we stop and enjoy the beauty of the glass. Humankind could perfectly enjoy the beauty of the glass before the fall, and in the new creation, we are told that there will be eternal feasting, but in this in-between stage of mosaic patterns, we have the opportunity to do both. We have the opportunity to join Jesus in times of fasting and lack, and we have the opportunity to join in the victory and glory from Jesus' resurrection.

Feasting is an act of faith. It is taking part in the belief that Jesus is working in us and in our world *now*. His work in pulling our world back together has already begun in a way that allows us to taste the future feast even before our bodies have been resurrected.

Feasting, however, does *not* look like an act of faith when it is all we do. Jumping from feast to feast, playing a sort of "don't step on the crack" game with fasting is a surefire way of ridding ourselves from ever feasting at all. A person who always eats rich food can never appreciate the simplicity of a raw vegetable. And so, when offered raw food, this person finds him- or herself unsatisfied and disappointed. In the same way, a Christian who only ever dwells on the glories and joys of our life here on earth will have a very hard time comprehending—or even surviving—seasons of trials that come.

Church traditions like Lent and Easter provide patterns for the believer, intentional times to dwell on both the brokenness and the miraculousness. This is the beauty of the mosaic. We take time to fast, pausing to stay connected with the reality of our world, and then we take time to feast, pausing to rejoice in the gifts and glories that are with us today and those which are coming for us in the future.

Jesus himself walks this balance of fasting and feasting. He is fasting from the fruit of the vine until we come, and he is also seated at the right hand of the Father in heaven. He has defeated death, and yet he is also pausing before he returns to abolish evil once and for all. He experiences joy and delight when he watches his children on the earth thrive, and he mourns and grieves when he sees us in pain. Jesus is an example to the Christian of how to live on this mosaic, and to be a Christian is to follow in his example.

This mosaic will color our entire lives. We will have times for feasting and times for mourning. Each of these seasons comes with challenges and rewards, and it is up to us how we will receive them.

> I have learned in, whatever situation I am, to be content. I know how to be brought low, and I know how to abound. In any and every circumstance, I have learned the secret of facing plenty and hunger, abundance and need. I can do all things through him who strengthens me. (Philippians 4:11–13)

Faith is required both in times of abundance and in times of lack. Remembering where our true hope lies is much harder when we are used to having all of our earthly needs around us. But as it says in the passage above, we can do all of these things when Christ strengthens us. His empowerment is the only component required for thriving both in times of plenty and in times of want.

Why Feast?

For the Feaster, it comes as second nature to feast. On Thanksgiving Day, we show up at the designated house of hosting with a pair of stretchy pants, to-go containers, and about five dishes that we insisted on making ourselves because we wanted the food done *just* the way we like it. Feasters aren't just lovers of food; we are lovers of *good* things, and we are not ashamed to admit it.

Feasters like me aren't necessarily gluttons, though we can err that way. We simply have the natural knack and inclination to find ways to be happy. We are those hopscotching, leaping from glass pane to glass pane, being sure not to trip over anything unpleasant. When feast time comes, we sing the loudest and plan the hardest to maximize all opportunities for happiness. This is a good thing. The world needs us Feasters to remind everyone to stop and, yes, to smell the roses.

For the Faster, it is not as simple. For some, rejoicing is not the easy thing to do; the brokenness or darkness in our world can easily overwhelm and suffocate even God's children. The Faster appreciates the music in minor keys and the sermons about death. Focus on the "grout lines" gives them assurance that God isn't just concerned with us trying to be happy, but he is aware of the real state of things. They need to know that there is a place for their tears, a value to their concerns, and a need for their perspective. These are the Christians who may struggle to know how to approach a feast.

"Sing," we tell them. "Dance! Jesus is risen! Hallelujah!"

This last Easter, which I described above, was one of my first times seeing the world through the eyes of the Faster. People yelling out "Hallelujah!" as they smiled seemed discordant, almost unkind.

"What about people like me?" I felt the urge to yell, "I don't *get* to say hallelujah!"

The truth is, I *do* get to sing hallelujah. In fact, I am *told* to sing hallelujah (for instance, in Psalm 113).[3] Despite the pain in my body and inability to eat solid food—despite the oxymoron on my lips as I yell the words—it is what I am *supposed* to do.

Part of being a follower of Christ is being led to places we don't always want to go. Sometimes we love the path, and sometimes we hate it. The Feaster loves feast time, and the Faster feels jarred by it. The Faster appreciates fast time, and the Feaster is agonized by it. All Christians are led through the rhythm of fasting and feasting, and it does good for all of us.

We all experience this broken world differently, but as the church we all walk together, both on the grouting and the glass. We each need the other spurring us on, whether through the fast or through the feast.

Feasting Is a Foretaste

But the feast must always come. The feast is the prize for which we prepare. It is a pearl of great price that is worth selling everything we have. We all strive through life on this earth so that we may taste the fullness of the glory to come! Feast days force us to connect with our future. They are a foretaste of the food that is to be served to us when we finally unite with Christ in the flesh.

When Israel as a nation finally conquered Jericho and moved into the promised land, they were told to continue the feasts and practices they had been given after their exodus from Egypt. Why? They were told to feast in order to *remember* how they got where they were. The feasting and fasting rhythms that Israel practiced as a nation were reminders of who they were as a people—past, present, and future.

Feasting does this for us, too. We would forget about the startling reality that God became human if we did not remind ourselves tangibly every Christmas, and we would forget about the reality of our approaching resurrection if we did not celebrate Easter.

If we don't feast, then we have no reminder of why we work so hard, what we are waiting for, and that this hardship is destined to end. Without feasts, our day-to-day lives reflect something *other* than reality to us. We feast in order to remind ourselves not just intellectually but tangibly that more *is* coming. It is *true*, Christian! More is coming! Hallelujah!

My job is to shout hallelujah, even when I don't feel it. My generation proudly debunked the whole fake-it-till-you-make-it mentality, labeling it as unhealthy thinking. That's fine. But let's coin a new term: *do-it-because-it's-true*. Our feelings are very subjective, and they're very often hard to control. But as I have been learning in my pain therapy, what we think and what we do can help guide our feelings. Thinking, doing, and feeling are all ways in which we respond to the world we live in, and they influence one another.

While sermons might help us cognitively interact with our faith, and prayer might help us emotionally connect with our God—behavioral interactions also greatly inform our experience with Jesus. Things we think change us; things we feel change us; and things we do change us. This is why we submit all of these things to God as Christians. To follow Christ is to believe that there is someone bigger than us who is forming us, and if we submit to his guidance, we will thrive.

Like fasting, feasting is a physical way of letting a truth that is bigger than ourselves form us. Though I don't feel like rejoicing, I still say hallelujah; and though all I ever do is fast, I still enter into the season of Lent with my family. Remember, feasting is a foretaste. We will not taste the real feast until heaven. No, these foretastes are meant to help us develop an appetite for what is to come. They teach us what to long for.

On my thirteenth birthday, I found an abandoned baby animal. It was pink and only just born. I saw no mother nearby, so I brought it into the house and tried to nurse it back to health. I fed it milk through a syringe, and by some strange miracle, it survived! It took us a while to deduce what sort of animal it was. It looked like nothing we had ever seen: a long skinny body, a tail with a black tip, and the cutest little sea-lion face. It wasn't a squirrel; it wasn't a chipmunk. What was it?

I fed her milk until she began to grow into a more defined shape. Finally, I was able to identify her as an ermine—a long-tailed weasel. A bit of research showed me that the little animal was a carnivore, incidentally the smallest of all carnivores. I therefore tried feeding her tuna from a can. She ate it up so quickly, you would have thought she was starving. The second it was gone, she walked over to her heated rice bag and bit into it, refusing to let go. We tried picking her up, and she pulled the rice bag with her; she was not letting go! We all laughed, and I remember my mom saying, "Well, she has developed the taste for meat, and now she has realized she is a hunter."

This is a silly illustration, but I still have that image in my mind: that tiny little weasel dragging around that massive, heavy rice bag, all because she wanted to chomp into something. Before trying meat, she had been happy with milk. But after her taste for meat had been triggered, she would be satisfied by nothing else.

This is what feasts do for Christians. It whets our appetites and teaches us to crave what is coming in the future. Friends, we are *supposed* to feel dissatisfied! When I threw up most of what I ate on Easter Sunday, I was *supposed* to feel the longing for more. It is good to find contentment with the road Jesus leads us on, yes—even though it may include suffering and hardship. But we are also called to be *discontent* with the sin and brokenness around us. Feasts give us that "taste for meat," giving us the *feeling* of being whole and the desire for the real thing—for complete righteousness. We celebrate Christ's resurrection, knowing that resurrection is what is coming for us.

The True Feast

This is why I love communion so much. Communion is *literally* giving us the taste for blood. Week by week, we are tasting Jesus' blood and eating his body. We are developing the taste for the man who holds the keys to true wholeness, true righteousness, and true contentment.

Our future isn't just feasts, whole bodies, and perfection. The future we are taught to long for is life in the presence of Jesus Christ. If we are seeking him, serving him, and tasting him week by week through communion, we are training ourselves to want the only true feast: Jesus Christ himself.

Jesus is our feast! He is the prize we receive. Heaven holds an eternal life with the Source of our salvation. And while he is already with us in Spirit, yes, he is also in heaven. He is our feast, but we don't have him—not fully, not yet! We await his return, knowing that once we are reunited, we will finally be whole. If we were wholly content here on this earth, right now, something would be wrong. We are *missing* something. We are waiting earnestly for something. We are being *taught* to crave him because, otherwise, we might forget what life is truly about!

> Now John's disciples and the Pharisees were fasting. And people came and said to him, "Why do John's disciples and the disciples of the Pharisees fast, but your disciples do not fast?" And Jesus said to them, "Can the wedding guests fast while the bridegroom is with them? As long as they have the bridegroom with them, they cannot fast. The days will come when the bridegroom is taken away from them, and then they will fast in that day." (Mark 2:18–20)

Think about it: Before Jesus, his people fasted; while Jesus was on the earth, his disciples did not fast; and now that he is back in heaven, his people are fasting again. This passage perfectly captures the reason why we feast and the reason why we fast. Both rituals remind us of what it is we are waiting for. Fasting reminds us of how much we are truly longing for wholeness, and feasting reminds us that good *is* coming.

In my situation, I need to strike a balance between these two things in order to navigate the road of suffering. Fasting reminds me that I am broken and I *will* suffer in this life. It helps me stay aware of my weakness and my need for salvation. Feasting reminds me that I *will* be made whole—this suffering *will* end. God may be doing good in me *through* my suffering, but he also wants to end it for *good*! Both of these things need to be true in order for me not to turn to the right or to the left. I keep my eyes on Jesus as I look to the cross for guidance amid my pain, and I keep my eyes on the resurrected Jesus, fighting for the moment when I am whole like he is whole.

And that's it, right there. This is the goal for which we are striving. Fasting is meaningless if there is no future feast. I emphasize fasting for an entire book only so that I can end the book with the biggest exclamation point—the shrillest scream and the loudest shout: *Jesus is coming back!*

I am fasting because *he* isn't *here*. His Spirit is with me, yes, and his word is transforming me, yes. *But something is missing.* This is the story that my suffering, my starvation, and my dying body is telling: He isn't here. His work is *not* finished!

If I could yell through the pages, I would. If I could declare, "My suffering is not meaningless!" from every mountaintop and rooftop, I would. If my suffering led to nothing, then I am nothing but an object of pity. But that's the thing—this is the point where my entire book rests. It is the ultimatum; it is the moment where you either believe all of it or none of it. This is the moment when you as a reader either pity or rejoice over me. There is no middle ground here; you either believe it or you don't. And here it is: *My hope rests on a future resurrection.* The apostle Paul said it best:

> Now if Christ is proclaimed as raised from the dead, how can some of you say that there is no resurrection of the dead? But if there is no resurrection of the dead, then not even Christ has been raised. . . . And if Christ has not been raised, your faith is futile and you are still in your sins. Then those also who have fallen asleep in Christ have perished. If in Christ we have hope in this life only, we are of all people most to be pitied. . . . If the dead are not raised, "Let us eat and drink, for tomorrow we die." (1 Corinthians 15:12–13, 17–19, 32)

Friends—this *has* to be true. The future resurrection really is coming. Jesus really did rise from the dead. If it is not true, then everything I have fought for is meaningless. Why give up alcohol? Why live each day in pain? Why take communion? Why strive for righteousness? If this final exclamation point isn't true—if Jesus didn't rise from the dead, and if he isn't going to raise us from the dead—then this book might as well be thrown into the trash. *Everything*—all my hope; all my endeavors; all my sanity—is all placed on the risen Christ.

This is the axis on which my entire life turns: Do I believe this? Or don't I?

I have been forced to face this question. I live in a body so acquainted with brokenness that I must either give in to the pain or give in to the resurrection. Do I despair, or do I hope? In a world with no resurrection, what is happening to me is a tragedy. Oh, how sad. A young mother with four children who can no longer eat. *Her* children are forced to listen to her vomiting several times a day; *her* artistic career will be damped by her shaking hands; her pain must feel like meaningless torture. Oh, what a tragedy!

If there is no resurrection, then someone like me should be pitied, because this is the only chance for life that I will ever have.

There is no other life for me, so I should just eat, drink, and make myself merry. I should drown myself in whatever momentary pleasures are offered to me.

But what if Jesus really did rise from the dead? What if that man two thousand years ago really was crucified, only to be raised? What if he promised to raise anyone else who followed in his footsteps?

If this is true, then I am so, so blessed. I am one of those shining children of God who chose to be made new by their suffering, like silver in the crucible. Pounded between the hammer and anvil of discipline and hope, I am one of the pure ones. I am the luckiest. My suffering kept me focused—it kept me clinging to the only life that has ever been offered to anyone in this world.

You see, all this theology about new bodies really is true. And if it isn't, then nothing in this book really matters. This is true, friends—the biggest climax and the greatest victory of all victories: Jesus is coming back!

So when I stand in the congregation on Easter Sunday, singing songs that cry "he is alive" and "I am made new," I am like a lump of silver, looking upward as I am pounded into shape, reminding myself that I will one day be a ring on the hand of the king. I am hanging everything I have on this truth—on the truth we celebrate every single Easter: He is alive, and he is coming back to make us alive.

If you have come this far with me, my final question for you is this: Do you believe this? Do you *really* believe that he is coming back? Is all this suffering *really* worth it?

If you don't, then by all means: Eat, drink, and be merry, for you *will* die. Honestly, don't waste your time with righteousness; do not withhold any pleasure from yourself. If this really isn't true, then you should pity me—that poor woman, so young to suffer so much. If it really isn't true, then what I am going through really is that terrible; it really is hopeless. Poor Tasha.

But what if it *is* true? If it really is true, then my lifelong fast will bring the greatest yield of all. Like Job, whose worldly treasures doubled after his tragic losses, my treasures stored up in heaven will be many. My suffering will continue to grow and mature me, and while my fasting creates a hole of emptiness in my stomach in this life, it will at the same time fill a mountain of treasure in my eternal life with Christ.

I want to be the poster child of the foolish, suffering Christian who cries to the world: *Join me! I walk the road of the cross! Come this way; this way is life!* I want my life to be so radical—so foolish, according to the world—that it only makes sense if Jesus is raised, is coming back, and will give me a new body. I want to be the Christian that forces those around me to stop and think: *How? How has this woman not given into despair?*

My story is either a tragedy or an epic with a happy ending. What do you think? Am I to be pitied? Or am I one of the luckiest of all?

8

my new life

Amen

I can't wrap up this book, or my story, with a bow. I don't know what my life holds from here on out. I have kept many medical symptoms and details vague simply because the diagnostic journey changes week to week. Maybe I will be healed, and all these things will go away. Maybe my symptoms will completely change. I really don't know. But as I mentioned in my introduction, this book is a prayer. It is an ambition and a road map for how I plan to continue on.

It is a testimony to how God has been with me for the last year of loss, and it is a cry to God to continue to be with me. My life will change. I will be changed by God and also changed by my suffering. I don't know what will happen; all I know is whom to cling to. I am like a shipwrecked sailor, clutching at a life raft amid the storm. While Jesus gives me strength to cling on, I will not let go.

Choosing the New Life

How is life now, as I finish writing this book? It's hard. Really hard. We are fragile in ourselves, but we feel strong in our faith; we feel completely destabilized in our life, but we are clinging on to the stability of who Jesus is; we are struggling with the road set before us, but we are trusting in the risen Lord. My body experiences constant pain and continual breakdown, but my *soul* is thriving.

I am trying very hard not to say that "we are okay." I don't really know what being "okay" means—it is far too subject to interpretation.

I like to use the word "*thriving*" instead, because it encompasses so much more than momentary feelings. Is my body dying—is *everyone's* body dying? Yes. Yet, with this decaying body, I am thriving. This, I believe, is what sets the Christian sufferer apart from everyone else who suffers: Our suffering does not add to our broken state; it adds to our soul health and our future resurrection. Our suffering is hopeful; each moment of pain is like an investment of gold into our future life with Christ.

It is hard to suffer, yes, but suffering acts as a healthy reminder of where to invest my time and my hope. My suffering has forced me into a state of sobriety and vigilance. Like Charles Dickens' character Scrooge, I have been forced to see how little time I really have. Some may say that it's cruel to show a young woman just how close death is, but I see it as a kindness. I see how much time I have wasted numbing myself and how much of my life I took for granted.

Like Scrooge waking up on Christmas morning with *joy* in his heart rather than terror at the reminder of how close he was to death, I have woken up on Christmas morning with clear sight and a thankful heart. Like Scrooge, I come to this chapter saying, "I have been changed by what I have been through, and I don't just want to be generous on Christmas Day: I want to treat every day like Christmas!"

It's inspiring, what happened to Scrooge—learning how to wake up and live his life for the better. But it's not easy to treat every day like Christmas. For me, every day that I wake up, before I even get out of bed, I am forced to decide: Will I choose to fast today?

Where We Are Now

Here is a little window into what our life looks like now. Lindsay works from home but travels for work here and there. I wake up, walk through the Daily Office prayer, take my pills, and assess where my pain is at. Pain dictates how much or little liquid I will be able to swallow without vomiting. I have a four-point scale to rate what sort of day I am having:

1. The pain and vomiting are more than what I am able to cope with. I am either on bed rest or in the hospital.
2. My pain and vomiting are under control but debilitating. I am not able to homeschool, and work output is low.
3. My symptoms are under control, and I am keeping to my daily routine of homeschooling, work, making dinner, etc.
4. I am experiencing less pain than usual, full of energy, and able to achieve big leaps in my projects. This will not last, and I must be aware that I should only do so much on a 4-point day.

Depending on what number I am that day, I align my expectations for myself. I have to be careful to stay on diet, not do too much, and not let my suffering step into the driver's seat and steer me out of control. My life is like walking a tightrope. I have to keep my eyes forward and stick with the plan. If I look right or left, I may fall. Still, I use constant prayer as my guardrails, keeping me from falling off the rope.

I go downstairs for family prayer, which takes only about ten minutes, but it gives our family a chance to connect before everyone goes about their day. After that, Lindsay and I get on the same page with how I am doing and how he is doing.

Then the day begins! I homeschool my four children, and if it's a 1 or 2 kind of day, I set them up with work they can do without me. After school, I am free to work on my projects, whether writing or drawing, and digging into God's word to mine for gems of wisdom. You can always find me in some kind of creative space during the latter part of the day, until it's time to make dinner.

It's a happy thing that I still can both write and draw when I am in pain. Whether at my drawing table or parked in bed, I've got an iPad on my lap. I illustrate for the FatCat series; I write books like this; and most often, I am writing fiction. *So* much fiction.

By five o'clock, I am back on mother duty. If I am able, I clean. If I am able, I make dinner. Sometimes I am able to squeeze in more writing time, but nowadays I try to see that as my chance to connect with the kids. After dinner and family time, we gather for evening prayer. We put the kids to bed, then Lindsay and I have some connection time, then I take my evening pills, and we go to sleep.

What a lovely life I have. Sure, I have to juggle pain, vomiting, exhaustion, vertigo, shaking hands, and so on—but still. Those things can happen while I live my life.

Feasting/Fasting Mindset

I may not be able to swallow solid food, but I can still choose whether or not to fill that lack with unfulfilling things. When I choose to fast, I am choosing to be the girl who doesn't eat solid food. Yes, despite my inability to swallow solid food, I can still try to fight against that reality and trick myself into thinking I don't really need to deprive myself.

So, when I fast, I am allowing lack to remain all throughout my day, trusting Jesus to be enough to fill the void. I wake up hungry every morning, and it is hard to fill that need with only liquid food. When I am not choosing to fast, I fight against my emptiness. I drink enough morning smoothie to feel "full," which then causes me to vomit, or I saturate my day with easy pleasures, like soft chocolates or take-out soups. When I swim upstream against my lack, I avoid the fast. I fight to be someone who indulges and feasts just so I don't have to face the emptiness. But when I let the fast carry me, like a boat down the river, I go the way Jesus leads me to go: the way of thriving.

Lindsay and I have developed a whole new perspective for our lives based on feasting and fasting. It's not just me who has to choose this fast each day. As Lindsay watches me suffer through an esophageal blockage or listens to me complain that I don't have as many treats as others do, he also has to trust that Jesus is enough for me. He, too, feels the pull to help fill my emptiness. What good husband *wouldn't* want to do this? When one of us isn't fasting, we create a drag on the little boat that is our marriage, which is trying to take us to a healthier place. When Lindsay is responding to his exhaustion by ordering Domino's pizza, it pulls me back to that old way of thinking: *I need more in order to be okay*. It's harder to fast when those around me are turning to their personal feasts for contentment.

This is why we started using the language of a feasting and fasting mindset. We realized that we have to turn our hearts toward satisfaction in order to live in a healthy way. We realized that our inclination to self-medicate with feasting didn't just affect how we ate but flavored every area of our lives.

Here is how we look at it: Living life with a feasting/fasting mindset is receiving as a gift that our life has periods of abundance (feasting) and periods of lack (fasting) and that both are good for us. There is good for us if we find contentment in both the feasting *and* the fasting. There is meaning in our times of fasting and meaning in our times of feasting, and if we press into this meaning, rather than resist it, we will receive gifts that are only accessible in those specific periods of time.

For example, I have had to give up alcohol most of the time, both because it counteracts some of my medications and also because I developed an unhealthy dependency on it. So, without any wine all week long, there really is only one time when I get to drink it: on Sundays during communion. Before I gave up wine, communion was just another sip in a long string of indulgences. But now, every Sunday, when I taste the communion port, it has suddenly become one of the greatest tastes of my life. It is finally in *truth* a weekly feast. I cannot have it any other day of the week; it is a feast reserved for Sunday.

If I ride the waves of fasting and feasting in my life, it produces meaning like this. Before, communion food seemed bland in comparison to the rest of my week, but now, I see a meaning in it that I had never seen before. I see this burst of flavor as a foretaste of the richness of my resurrection life to come.

We have started to weave this way of thinking into many aspects of our life. Sometimes this lens can be used to look at *specific periods of time*—for example, when our family of six lived in a two-bedroom apartment for a year as we waited to buy a house in the United States. This lens can also be used to look at a certain *aspect* of life that may or may not change. For example, I have friends my age who are still single, despite their desire to be married. To them, this feels like a seemingly unending fast for a heart that longs to be filled.

When we see our various rhythms and seasons of fasting and feasting as opportunities for meaning, it makes our lives much more beautiful. This perspective gives Christians motivation to slow down, look around, and soak up the day they are in. What if every day of the Christian life was like a day in the garden of Eden? What if each day, you woke up and looked around, seeing both gifts freely given and trees about which Jesus says, "*You cannot eat from that?*" What if you knew that every day Jesus would be in that garden with you, pointing out gifts and meaning available for that day? What if, in that garden, you knew that no matter what hardships or emptiness you face, Jesus will face them right alongside you?

Life doesn't seem so impossible this way, does it? The fasting/feasting mindset focuses us, giving us vigilance to face and accept our battles and hearts that are eager to accept the given gifts of each day. This mindset is transforming many areas of my family's life, and it has enabled us to press into whatever season we are in.

The first example I can think of is our finances. We have often used money as a Band-Aid for the many losses our circumstances have created. *Tasha is sad today because she went to a party where none of the food served was liquid enough for her to swallow, and now she has come home hungry not just for food, but for the feeling of a feast; that's okay! Let's buy her some liquid food that feels special! It doesn't matter if the delivery cost is just as high as the expensive dish: you can't put a price on making Tasha feel special on a night like this!* Or perhaps: *The kids are all crying because Mama was rushed off to hospital again. Mama is feeling bad to cause her children such sadness, and it is adding to her own burdens. It's okay! Mama can just buy some presents for the kids from Target and have it delivered the same day! That makes this day special!*

Now, you might be thinking: *I see no problem here! You shouldn't feel bad about either of those!* And I agree. I should not feel bad about those things on their own. Those were both very real, very recent, and very hard examples of past situations. But there are two things to keep in mind: In both of those circumstances, we did not have the budget for any extra spending, and we had to add to our debt in order to do them. And second, this sort of Band-Aid solution might be the right thing to do as a one-off, but it is not a sustainable form of comfort. This was a pattern in our life: to comfort ourselves with money, promising each other that it was "just this once."

The fasting/feasting mindset broke this pattern open and exposed it for what it really was: a form of gluttony. We *needed* to have our every need met. What if, we thought, we treated our money like we treat feasting and fasting? If we live according to our budget and only spend the allotted money each week, then we are fasting from buying anything else. Anything we don't have the budget for is inaccessible to us, and much like the Tree of the Knowledge of Good and Evil, it may look "good to eat," but we do not need it. Then, whenever we get extra money to spend on something special, it is a sort of feast, and we are able to rejoice in it after spending so much time saying no to other things.

In practice, this is hard but also rewarding. Yeah, it hurt to say no when we wanted to pick up Happy Meals for the kids on the way home from a late-night errand, but it also felt good. Like leaning against the glass of a lion exhibit at the zoo, it felt good to be safe. By fasting from spending, we were spared a hurried decision that would most likely have led to regret.

Pressing into the fast of saving our money made us more present with our current season. We chose to keep to our budget so that we could get out of debt after two years of treading water while I fought for my life. If we kept self-medicating through money, we would only hurt ourselves further. But by being present with our reality, it helped us know what we were fighting for. We weren't fighting for a momentary, fleeting feeling; we were fighting to thrive in our current circumstances and in God's presence.

The fasting/feasting mentality helps us live, day by day, inside our allotted season. For me, it helps me keep my eyes on the prize.

I walk a tightrope, yes. But this mentality, and all the decisions to stick to my plan, are like guardrails on either side of me, giving me something to lean on if I falter. And believe me, I falter often! If I am to thrive, I must remain present, receiving both the hardships and the comforts that Jesus has for me in this time.

A Road Map

Writing this book was my way of compiling everything I have learned into a road map. Each chapter represents a truth or nugget of wisdom that has helped me endure my suffering, which can, at many times, be intense. I still experience periods of stinging hunger that make me cry, or days when my hands are so shaky that I can't write or draw. These days will continue, and I need a way to weather them. Every day I struggle not to try to fill the void of my fast with mini-feasts—whether ice cream or unplanned spending—and my hope is that, whatever comes my way, Jesus will give me everything I need to not only weather these storms but to be transformed by them. I am not an object of cruel torture; I am a patient traveler, gathering whatever gems I can from the caves I travel through, knowing I am on my way to everlasting life.

I focused my chapters on God's promises. His promises are the key to my road map for life. They keep me on course. These are promises for every Christian, whether you are suffering, afraid of suffering, or watching another person suffer. All of these promises hinge on the truth that *Jesus is with me*:

1. *I am one with Christ:* Jesus made me part of his body. I am one with Jesus. If I am one with Jesus, then I will walk the road he has walked. Because Jesus suffered and fasted, I will suffer and fast too. And because Jesus died, I will die

too. And because Jesus resurrected with a new body, I will resurrect too. This unity with Christ promises me all the same rewards that he has received through his victories.

2. *Man does not live by bread alone:* Jesus is my source of life. Eating food and drinking water are not the true sources of life. If Jesus is not breathing life into me, moment by moment, I will die. Times of fasting remind me where my true source of life is. Times of fasting, therefore, are good.
3. *Communion*: Jesus is my food. I do not live by bread alone but by his word. Jesus is present with me in his body and blood. He is present with me in his word. When I receive communion, I am eating his word. This is my true source of life. Though my physical body is fading, my soul is thriving.
4. *Sitting in the void:* Jesus is the keeper of peace. When I leave the void of loss and emptiness rather than try to fill it with distraction and vice, I am able to receive true peace amid my lack. When I am present with him in the lack, I can receive the gifts he has for me.
5. *Staying awake:* Jesus stays awake with me. I am not alone in my loss, so I do not need to hide from it. He will give me everything I need to endure the trial without the pain traumatizing me. When I stay awake, I can be transformed. When I stay awake, I am able to reap the full reward.
6. *Finding contentment*: Jesus is enough. When I am present with him, I am able to receive the gifts he has for me. Today and each day, I have precious gifts to receive. I will have peace when I receive the gift he offers

me today, rather than wishing for the gift I wanted or expected.

7. *The future feast is real, and it is worth fighting for:* Jesus is the feast. He will give me what I need to persevere so that he can give me the gift of himself. Any lack, loss, or pain I endure in this life is an investment in the future feast. Lack itself is not the end goal—*fasting* is not the end goal. The reason for my periods of emptiness are fulfilled in a future feast that finally gives us the feeling of fullness. If the future feast was not real, then the loss really would be a tragedy. The future feast *is* real, and therefore my fasting is not in vain.

I do realize that I crafted this list based on a prayer (the Book of Common Prayer's prayer after communion, which I pray quite often), but I have also chosen to summarize it all in a prayer of my own. When I feel too tired to face the fast, or when despair claws at the corners of my mind, these are words that I can say out loud, in faith that they will change me and guide me. I don't have to perfectly *believe in them* or even *want* them. I just need to say them and trust that the same Spirit who raised Jesus from the dead is inside me, turning my faith into action. My prayer:

Father in Heaven, thank you for the gift of this day; I ask for faith to see you in it, the strength to face the hardships, and the eyes to recognize it as good.

Jesus, you say you are with me, even right now as I say these words. Help me to remember you are there and to look to you rather than to earthly comforts when today feels hard. I need you with me, whether I am sitting, standing, walking, or unable to do any of those. I need you, even when I forget I need you. Stay with me, Jesus, just as you promised you would.

Jesus, give me this day my daily bread. Give me everything I need. Even when I cannot eat, you promised me that you would give me everything I need. Give me the strength to be satisfied with the bread you have given me today: the bread of yourself. Help me say, "It is enough." Even as I feel my dying body break a little more this day, give me the eyes to see the life you give my spirit and the heart to rejoice in it.

Jesus, I choose to fast. In faith, knowing I will falter, I want to fast. I want to leave the gaps of lack open so that I might see your beauty in new ways. I want to trust you that you are the only source of true peace and comfort. I am scared of the emptiness; I am scared that when I set aside my earthly comforts, I will be met with true emptiness and silence. I am scared that, when I turn down the volume of gluttony and self-medication, I will realize that you are not there. Jesus, you are with me. Help me to be courageous enough to sit with you, so that I may be given true peace.

Jesus, you stay awake with me, even when I choose to fall asleep to my pain. You watch over me, guarding me, even when I refuse to face the reality of my hardships. Jesus, wake me up today. Give me the vigilance to be watchful and the drive to rouse myself when I feel the fatigue of perseverance setting in. I want the gems that are available only on this day. I want to see them when they come. I believe that they are worth the sting of whatever purifying pain I may feel by remaining sober.

Jesus, you are enough for me. Help me to be grateful for the good things you have given to me on this day, and close my eyes and heart to anything that you have not given to me. Align my heart to your will; guide my expectations and hopes; and remind me of your love for me when I feel disappointment. May the words "not my will but your will be done" be on my lips and enable my heart to believe that your will is better for me than my own.

Jesus, you are my portion. You are the true feast, and you are the greatest prize. I receive your Spirit today. And as I wait for our future reunion in the flesh, I choose to sit in the lack that you are in heaven, and I am on earth. For you, I wait. Whatever pain and loneliness that this day has, I wear them as a cloak of longing for you. I taste you in Spirit now, but one day, I will feast in our eternal reunion. You are worth this wait. You are my portion; you are my reward—you are my bread of life.

I choose to receive all you have for me today, with gladness and singleness of heart. I choose you today, Jesus. You are enough for me.

Amen.

Awake, O Sleeper

Reader, thank you for reading my story. It is humbling to think that someone like you took the time to get this far. It is a gift to me. Now, I would like to end with a gift for you. I don't know what sorts of suffering or death surround you. Are you close to someone in physical pain? Are you in physical pain yourself? Are you sitting in the loss of a child, or the loss of something you didn't think you could live without? Are you at a loss for words for how to talk about your trials, or a loss for encouragement when you hear a story like mine?

Friend, it is not for us to rescue ourselves or others from suffering. Compassion we can give, and exhortation we can offer, but rescue comes from only one source. I don't want this book to leave you feeling powerless. Instead, I want to hand you a weapon to wield or perhaps a cup of cold water to offer when you find yourself talking to a person, like me, who deals with daily emptiness.

Once or twice a week I will have an interaction with someone in my life, whether a cashier at a grocery store or a friend at church, where I find reason to mention that I cannot eat solid food. Their reaction is almost always the same: stupefaction. After checking to see if they heard me right and if I really meant what I said, a look of hopelessness appears on their face. This is the moment where the person begins to think about what it might be like to be me—the moment where compassion becomes confusion. The conversation usually ends with them saying something like, "Well, I don't know what to say, but I hope you get better."

This is honestly the place where most people end up when they try to process what my life is like now: *I don't know what to say, except I hope it goes away.* These words are not dismissive or uncaring. They come from loving, compassionate people who honestly just don't know what to offer aside from their sympathy.

This feeling of powerlessness isn't all bad. Friend, you *are* powerless to rescue a sufferer like me from my predicament. It's not your job to rescue anyone. There *is* a role you play, though, and in *that* sense, you are not powerless. Remember we are the church: the arms, legs, and vital parts of Christ's body here on earth. It is our job to speak truth to one another, exhorting each other to press on down the road of the cross. There are words and promises to give your brothers and sisters in Christ who are suffering—words like the ones I listed above in my road map.

It is your job to point the sufferer to the only true source of healing and comfort—and that is Jesus. Jesus holds everything your suffering friend needs, even if those needs don't include healing on this side of heaven.

I imagine standing at that checkout station, chatting with the cashier. They comment on my odd choices of food, and I mention my liquid-only diet. I see that look on their face twist, that look of confusion mixed with dread. Then I myself feel the loneliness of my road. It is a road that no one seems to have a hopeful imagination for.

Here is what that cashier could say to someone like me, if I could put words in their mouth: "*I am so sorry for the loss and pain you feel, but it is not in vain. Hold fast to Jesus: he has good in this for you today.*"

Do you cringe when you read that? Don't cringe. I want you to feel empowered. When you speak the words of truth, you wield the power of Christ. As your lips move, you impart the fiery vigilance of the Holy Spirit. When you speak truth to people like me, it is like a jolt of energy, refocusing our eyes on the prize ahead.

Friends, this road will not be easy. We will not always want to fast. We will walk in faith some days, and we will falter on others. We will be like Peter, walking on water, only to look away from Jesus—the only one who was keeping us afloat—and start to sink. Still, he will always be there to reach out his hand. He will always be there to rescue us when we cry, "Lord, save me!"

This is not only the story of my affliction; this is the Christian life. We are called to be like children, dependent on a Savior. We are called to remember that we are weak and we need help. Our road is not one of pulling up our bootstraps; it is one of focused dependency.

Let us commit and recommit ourselves to this road daily. Let us wake up every morning, remembering we need grace. Let us begin each day with a simple prayer, asking for God's presence.

I leave you with this last exhortation: All this sacrifice—all this sitting in the loss—is worth it. Don't wait. Don't tarry while your earthly comforts pull you further into the lie that they will relieve your suffering. Put away the distractions and find time to sit in the presence of God. Find out that he is sufficient—more sufficient than you thought he was.

It does not have to be daunting or scary starting down this road. It can start small. It could be as simple as saying the Lord's Prayer when you wake up in the morning, or taking communion with God's people every Sunday, or practicing small amounts of fasting.

But don't wait. Your suffering is real and deep. It deserves a treatment and remedy that is powerful enough to actually lead to your thriving. It deserves comfort that is proportionate to the severity of your pain, whether physical or otherwise. The comfort of Christ will not downplay your suffering; it will dignify it. The presence of Christ will not force you to be someone you are not; it will allow you to be more yourself. The promises of Christ will not tempt you with euphoria, only to disappoint; they will satisfy you. The gladness of Christ will not feel forced or fleeting; it will be lasting and genuine. The compassion of Christ does not pity, patronize, or belittle; it is profoundly honest and dignifying.

Taste, Christian—taste and see that the Lord is good. Hold fast, sufferer; your trials are not in vain. Take heart, O weary one; there is rest for you. I have been to the lion's den, and I have been inside the fiery furnace. I know how scary it can be; I know how hopeless it can feel. But just like God's people inside the lion's den and the fiery furnace, I was not—I am not—alone. You are not alone.

And as Paul says in Ephesians, "Awake, O sleeper, and arise from the dead, and Christ will shine on you" (Ephesians 5:14). You do not need to be afraid of the road you walk. You may step out into the light without fearing anything. He is with you.

notes

1. Chosen Lack

1. Jean-Claude Larchet, *The Theology of Illness*, trans. John Breck and Michael Breck (St. Vladimir's Seminary Press, 2002), 10.

2. Larchet, *The Theology of Illness*, 10.

3. By Bread Alone

1. Basil the Great, "First Homily on Fasting," in *On Fasting and Feasts*, trans. Susan R. Holman and Mark DelCogliano, Popular Patristics 50 (St Vladimir's Seminary Press, 2013), 3.

2. Horatio Spafford, "It Is Well with My Soul."

4. Temptation to Compensate

1. Isaac the Syrian, *Ascetic Discourse* 5, quoted in Larchet, *The Theology of Illness*, 65.

2. Gregory of Nazianzus, *Letters* 31.2–3, quoted in Larchet, *The Theology of Illness*, 58.

3. John Chrysostom, *Homilies on John* 38, quoted in Larchet, *The Theology of Illness*, 63.

4. John Chrysostom, *Homily on the Paralytic* 2, quoted in Larchet, *The Theology of Illness*, 61–62.

5. Staying Awake

1. Christopher Cook, host, *Win Today*, podcast, episode 282, "Jamie Winship on Getting Unstuck," February 23, 2022.

2. Christopher Cook, host, *Win Today*, podcast, episode 282, "Jamie Winship on Getting Unstuck," February 23, 2022.

7. Feasting

1. *The Lord of the Rings: The Two Towers*. Directed by Peter Jackson. 2002. USA: New Line Cinema. Film.

2. Larchet, *The Theology of Illness*, 33.

3. "Hallelujah" is often translated "praise the Lord." So where Scripture says to sing praises to the Lord, it's literally telling us to say "hallelujah"!

Natasha Kennedy is an author and illustrator based in Seattle. She is passionate about the relationship between art and theology and enjoys sharing the beauty and truth of Christ with the world through her work. Natasha suffers from several debilitating chronic illnesses and an invisible disability that causes her chronic pain and prohibits her ability to eat. She is married to her husband, Lindsay, homeschools her four children, and has three cats, Curtains, Fauxe, and Fuzzy.

Connect with Natasha:

Kozmos.design

Facebook @Natashakennedu

Instagram @Natashakennedu

Twitter @Natashakennedu